BAHAMAS BUCKET LIST FOR DIVERS

BIMINI EDITION

BY CAPT. NATHAN RILEY

BAHAMAS BUCKET LIST FOR DIVERS: BIMINI EDITION

1405 SW 6th Avenue • Ocala, Florida 34471 • Phone 352-622-1825 • Fax 352-622-1875
Website: www.atlantic-pub.com • Email: sales@atlantic-pub.com
SAN Number: 268-1250

Library of Congress Cataloging-in-Publication Data

Names: Riley, Nathan, 1975- author.
Title: Bahamas bucket list for divers : Bimini edition / by: Nathan Riley.
Description: Bimini Edition. | Ocala, Florida : Atlantic Publishing Group,
    Inc., [2017] | Includes bibliographical references.
Identifiers: LCCN 2017022358 (print) | LCCN 2017031875 (ebook) | ISBN
    9781620234235 (ebook) | ISBN 9781620234228 (alk. paper) | ISBN 162023422X (alk.
    paper)
Subjects: LCSH: Diving--Bahamas--Guidebooks. | Diving--Bahamas--Miscellanea.
    | Diving--Bimini Islands--Guidebooks. | Diving--Bimini
    Islands--Miscellanea. | Bahamas--Guidebooks. | Bimini Islands
    (Bahamas)--Guidebooks.
Classification: LCC GV838.4.B34 (ebook) | LCC GV838.4.B34 R55 2017 (print) |
    DDC 797.2/34097296--dc23
LC record available at https://lccn.loc.gov/2017022358

Printed in the United States

PROJECT MANAGER: Lisa McGinnes • lmcginnes@atlantic-pub.com
INTERIOR LAYOUT: Nicole Sturk • nicolejonessturk@gmail.com

Marta, Jordan, Xavier and Casie: thank you for allowing me
to plunder the sea and for sharing your lives with me.
—Nate

ACKNOWLEDGEMENTS

Thank You: Hank, Barb, Al, and my Bahamian mother, Saralee Pinder, for all your input over the years and over beers, and for being such gracious hosts – you truly represent the Bahamas and Bimini well. Natty "Piccolo Pete" Saunders, for the rum sessions. Kelly Melillo Sweeting and Kat DeStefano, AKA The Dolphin Girls, whose contribution was above and beyond. My mom and stepdad for giving me the first taste of boat life. The Bahamas Ministry of Tourism and all the beautiful residents who embody the spirit of the islands. Gwenda Ward, for being the teacher of a lifetime! Liza Hash, for not hating me as much as you thought you would. My esteemed shipmates Liz Czok, Amanda Kirk, Jimmy Miller, and John Beltromo, dive live-aboard legend. Also Debi Moir and the rest of the gang on the "Friends of Juliet" Facebook page.

Last and certainly not least: Mike Beach, Rusty Wright, Jackson Dozier, Sean Hartry, Rob Guarino, and Pete Watkins. There ain't no party like a . . . you scoundrels know the rest.

Over the years, we have adopted a number of dogs from rescues and shelters. First there was Bear and after he passed, Ginger and Scout. Now, we have Kira, another rescue. They have brought immense joy and love not just into our lives, but into the lives of all who met them.

We want you to know a portion of the profits of this book will be donated in Bear, Ginger and Scout's memory to local animal shelters, parks, conservation organizations, and other individuals and nonprofit organizations in need of assistance.

– Douglas & Sherri Brown,
President & Vice-President of Atlantic Publishing

TABLE OF CONTENTS

INTRODUCTION

*H*ave you envisioned embarking on that dream scuba adventure to an unexplored area of the Bahamas, but put it off due to uncertainty over which dive operation to choose? My name is Capt. Nathan Riley and I am here to tell you that your troubles are a thing of the past. If you're an enthusiastic diver looking for the perfect spot to test your diving skills, look no further than *Bahamas Bucket List for Divers: Bimini Edition* for information that will more than meet your needs.

Bahamas Bucket List for Divers: Bimini Edition will give you all the information that you will need to choose the dive operation that meets your requirements to suit your pleasure. It doesn't matter if you're a dive enthusiast looking to disconnect from the white noise and hustle and bustle of your day-to-day life, or a beginner just getting your feet wet. This guide will immerse you in the islands' rich culture, natural endowments, and soul. From pristine coral reefs to haunting wrecks, and even organized shark feeds, the islands' regal aquatic compositions are lying there, just waiting to be explored.

As a boat captain of 15 years, I've dived the Bahamas almost on a daily basis and have sought out and explored some of the greatest dives you can possibly find on the ancient island. This book will be your travel and marine life guide, while giving you a glimpse into Bimini's piratical history, which includes folktales, myths, and legends. It will give you insight into why this area is the tourist destination it is today. It also acts as a dive logbook for you to check off dive sites on your Bahamas bucket list; eventually, you can score yourself and find out just how much of a legendary aquatic daredevil you really are.

This guide will also put you in touch with areas accessed by the best dive operations, from land-based and live-aboard operators, depending on your interests. If you follow the directions in this book, you will find remote and pristine coral reefs, and organized shark feeds – including one of the only two known hammerhead aggregations in the world. The pages in this book will educate and enlighten you with in-depth knowledge on Bahamian island life and culture, all while acting as a store house for your favorite dive memories. As a dive log, it also enables you to check off dive sites along your journey.

The Bimini edition of this series is near and dear to me personally, perhaps because it is where I began my life and journey as a captain. It was a true labor of love putting this entire project together, and I hope it leads you to the scuba vacation that will give you a lifetime of memories to cherish. You're not going to forget this easily; I guarantee it.

GETTING TO BIMINI

For those with an adventurous soul, one way to get to Bimini is by the live-aboard dive boat *Juliet*. She is a schooner that is full of classic charm and is fully dive-functional. She operates from Miami to Bimini during the months of March through November. *Juliet* offers safe parking for the week for only $35 (at the time of publication).

When you arrive, you'll be greeted by a courteous and professional crew. Once you are aboard and checked-in, the *Juliet* will provide you with lunch, and on a typical day, will depart around 3 p.m.

As you get underway and departing through Government Cut, with the bow pointing into the Gulf Stream and the last channel marker behind you, there will be no doubt in your mind that you're on a great adventure. You'll watch the mania and manufactured glitz of Miami drop off the horizon.

The crew of the *Juliet* clears customs for you the morning following your departure and will have your dive adventure ready almost instantly. *Juliet* typically schedules up to four dives a day with three meals and snacks in between. All meals and alcohol are included in the cost, as well as dive tanks, dive briefings, and excellent service from the crew to make your stay enjoyable. *Juliet* also has nitrox and professional instructors on board, so if you would like to take your dive certification to another level, you can complete all checkout services onboard. There are additional costs involved, but it is well worth it!

One of the biggest advantages to diving from the *Juliet* is she has no set itinerary. She will go to any lengths within the realm of weather and safety to assure you have the most amazing dive adventure possible. Whether it's hitting the fan favorites of the Bimini area, or going all the way south to pristine Orange Cay and the Santaren Channel, if you're a dive enthusiast, the *Juliet* is one of the best ways to get a superb and comprehensive Bimini dive experience.

FLIGHTS

There are flights to Bimini from Ft. Lauderdale and Miami. Just remember Bimini is divided into two islands: north and south. The airport is on the south island, so if you're staying on the north island you'll have to take a taxi and ferry to get there. The price varies, but is usually under $20 for both. Just a heads up: the flights are short so don't expect 747 cabin service with drinks and snacks. The following airlines offer service from the U.S. mainland:

Cape Air

Phone: (800) 227-3247
Website: www.capeair.com
Service: To North Bimini Seaplane Base from FLL four times daily, and from Miami (Watson Island Seaplane Base) twice daily

Flamingo Air

South Bimini Airport, Bimini
Phone: (242) 347-4300
Website: www.flamingoairbah.com

Silver Airways

South Bimini Airport, Bimini
Phone: (242) 347-3124, (242) 347-4122
Email: info@silverairways.com
Website: www.gosilver.com

Sky Bahamas

South Bimini Airport, Bimini
Phone: (242) 347-4029
Website: www.skybahamas.net

Tropic Ocean Airways

Resorts World, North Bimini
Phone: (800) 767-0897, (954) 210-5569
Email: reservations@flytropic.com
Website: www.flytropic.com

Western Air

South Bimini Airport, Bimini
Phone: (242) 347-4100
Email: info@westernairbahamas.com
Website: www.westernairbahamas.com

WHERE TO STAY

The idea behind this guide is to put you in touch with the islands' culture and soul. Bimini's industry is inherently tied to its surrounding waters. A majority of the area hotels have marinas that face the pristine protected bay. A beautiful sunrise can be seen every morning, and to catch the sunset it's literally just a short walk across the street. I spent many days enjoying both. Most hotels are located right near the Alice Town straw market. Anything you could possibly need is within a short walk, whether it is groceries, fishing tackle, or beer. Any one of the following hotels will have you on the path to relaxation from the moment you arrive.

Weech's Dock and Bay View Rooms

Located on the south end of Alice Town with a stunning view of the harbor.

Phone: (242) 347-3028
Fax: (242) 347-3508
Address: P.O. Box 613, Bimini, Bahamas

SeaCrest Hotel and Marina

Located in Alice Town, Bimini. All rooms here offer ocean- or bay-view rooms so every view is great. A mini-fridge, TV, and air conditioning are also standard.

Phone: (242) 347-3071
Fax: (242) 347-3495
Address: P. O. Box 654, Bimini, Bahamas

Bluewater Marina

Located in Alice Town, Bimini. Blue Water Marina provides optimum comfort at one of the finest marinas in the Bahamas. Friendly staff are eager to make your visit a pleasurable one. Bimini Blue Water Marina is a veritable yachtsman's paradise located amidst some of the world's finest fishing.

Contact: Ms. Lisa Saunders
Phone: (242) 347-3166, (242) 347-3291
Fax: (242) 347-3293, (800) 688-4752
Email: biminibluewater@hotmail.com

The Big Game Club

Founded in 1947, The Big Game Club has hosted veritable anglers and visitors from all corners of the world. There is a restaurant on location and pool. It has 75 slips, and is capable of accommodating yachts up to 140 feet in overall length and has a 9-foot mean low water. The Big Game Club is at the very north end of Alice Town.

Reservations: (800) 867-4764

TOURS, ACTIVITIES, & OPERATORS

Here is a directory of outfitters with local knowledge that can put you on the path to adventure while you enjoy your stay in Bimini. Remember that you are on "island time." You will find everyone in Bimini will treat you like family.

Al Sweeting, Jr.

One of the best tour guides on the island for snorkeling, dolphins, stingrays, and reef sharks. In fact, he has been a great friend and host to many people over the years. He is "The Ultimate Bimini Tour Guide."

Contact Information: Captain Al Sweeting
Alice Town
Bahamas
Phone: (242) 347-3477

Neal Watson, Jr.

Neal is your guy if you're looking to dive in the Bimini area. He can put you onto a range of sites and adventures from reefs, coral walls, stingray groups, and the Hammerhead Safari when in season.

Contact Information: Neal Watson, Jr.
Toll Free (800) 867-4764
US (954) 615-1011
Local (242) 473-8816
neal@biminiscubacenter.com

SharkLab

Here is the place you can learn everything you ever wanted to know about the local shark species. They have been running the world's leading and longest-running study, and they are the leading research base on sharks in the Caribbean. They offer tours for a suggested $10 donation.

Contact Information: SharkLab
15 Elizabeth Dr., 05, Bimini
Phone: (242) 347-4538
VHF #88a

Bimini Museum

Not only a huge resource for this book, but a wonderful place to spend an afternoon, the Bimini Museum is on the top story of the original post-office above the old jail in Alice Town. It was restored in 1921 and is host to many artifacts, from cannons to Hemingway photos to Martin Luther King, Jr.'s immigration card. Donations are accepted and appreciated, and the museum is open during daylight hours. It's just a short walk from the ferry dock.

Contact Information: Sir Michael & Barbara Checkley
(242) 347-3038

Bonefish Tommy

Bonefish Tommy is a Bimini native who has probably forgotten more about fishing than most people ever know. His decades of experience will certainly have you landing one amazing adventure. He also offers mangrove tours.

Contact Information: Mr. Tommy Sewell
Phone: (242) 347-3234 or (242) 473-1089

Bonefish Ebbie

A certified bonefish guide with decades of experience, Ebbie will take to you where the fish are and share some laughs along the way. Mangrove tours also available.

Contact Information: Bonefish Ebbie
King's Highway, Porgy Bay, BI
(242) 347-2053

Ansil Saunders

Often regarded as the grandfather of bonefishing, he has boasted of clients such as the late Martin Luther King, Jr. He is a fly and light tackle expert and also a boat builder. He offers guided fishing charters, mangrove tours, and tours of his boat workshop.

Contact Information: Ansil Saunders
Phone: (242) 347-2178 or (242) 347-3098

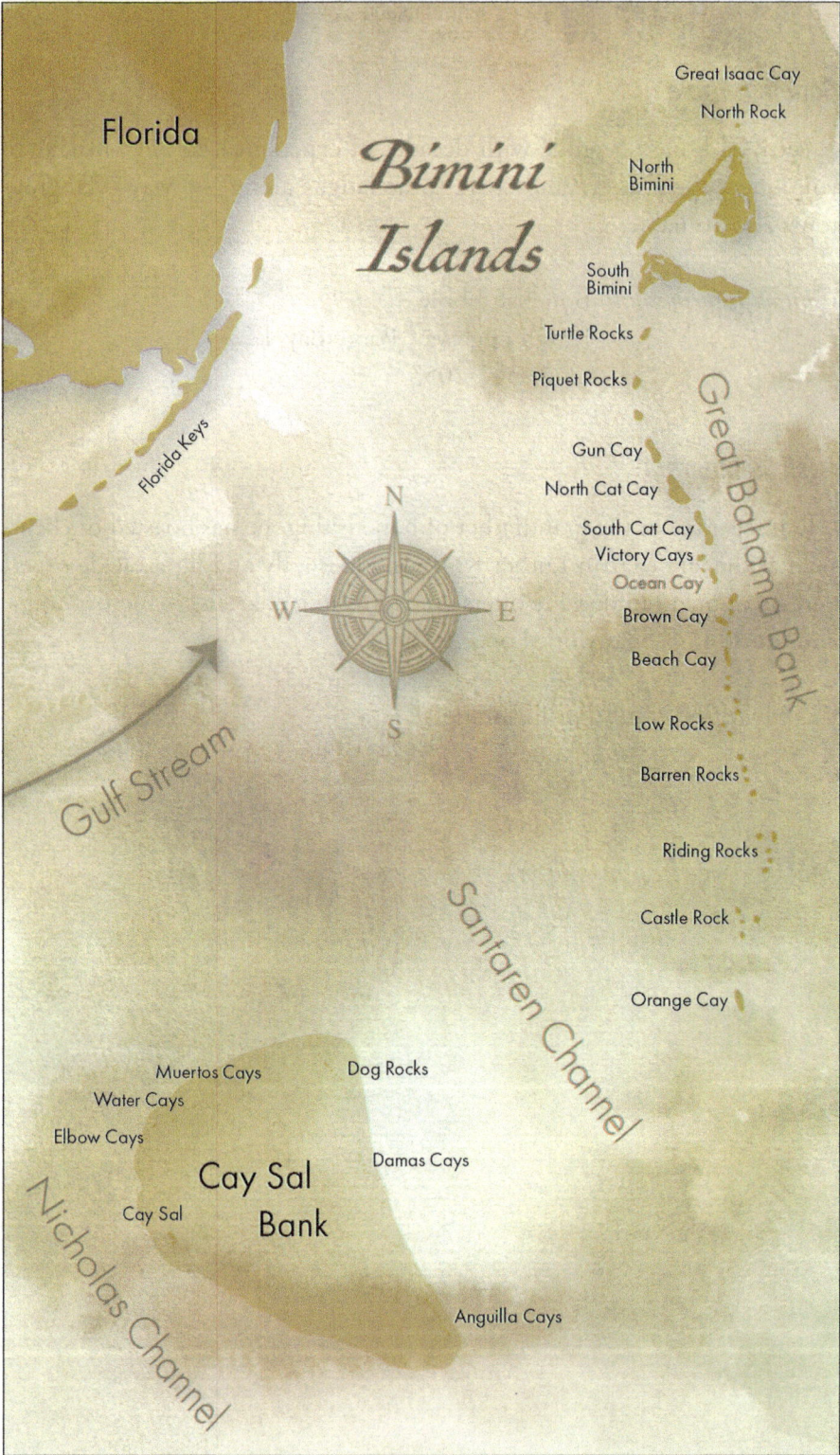

Florida

Bimini Islands

Great Isaac Cay
North Rock
North Bimini
South Bimini
Turtle Rocks
Piquet Rocks
Gun Cay
North Cat Cay
South Cat Cay
Victory Cays
Ocean Cay
Brown Cay
Beach Cay
Low Rocks
Barren Rocks
Riding Rocks
Castle Rock
Orange Cay

Great Bahama Bank

Florida Keys

Gulf Stream

Santaren Channel

Nicholas Channel

Muertos Cays
Water Cays
Elbow Cays
Cay Sal

Dog Rocks

Cay Sal Bank

Damas Cays

Anguilla Cays

N
W   E
S

Chapter 1

TINY ISLAND, BIG HISTORY

*B*imini is actually a combination of two islands divided into the north and south sides. It is located 45 nautical miles due east of the city of Miami, Florida and 120 nautical miles west of Nassau, the Bahamian capital. The two islands that comprise Bimini are separated by a beautiful bay. Just to the west, the northbound current known as the Gulf Stream is literally just off its doorstep, and it is flanked by the Great Bahama Bank to the east. Bimini has often found itself in the crosshairs of major historical occurrences. Its earliest settlers were mostly the Lucayan and Arawak Indians who lived a simple, peaceful life, subsisting on indigenous crops and fishing. The word "Bimini" translates to "two islands" in the Arawak language.

In 1492, Christopher Columbus took a famed voyage cutting across the Atlantic. This route led Columbus straight to the Bahamas and it is believed that he also landed on the island of San Salvador. It is pretty well-documented that Columbus was not that great a navigator, but nations were turning to the vast expanse of sea in an aim to expand their empires, territories, and wealth.[1]

---

1. Gerace, 1987

Legend Has It

Many locals believe that in the 1500s, Ponce De Leon landed on Bimini during his famed and ultimately failed quest for the fountain of youth. Today, the Healing Hole that was discovered by De Leon is a popular park and tourist attraction on the way to the airport on South Bimini. After a brief stop in Bimini, Ponce De Leon moved on with his quest, and Bimini existed quietly as history was evolving, about to greatly erupt around it yet again.

The first big catalyst that would forever change the Bahamas was the end of the War of Spanish Succession. With the end of this war, thousands of sailors found their wages were greatly cut or they were suddenly without a job. They tried to make do in careers as merchant sailors, but with the market continuously flooded with trained mariners, wages were spread thin. It was a simple case of supply and demand. The Bahamas would soon end up a haven for pirates.

Military vessels often had crews consisting of the poor, prisoners, or slaves. The officers ruled with iron fists and the captain was absolute in his authority. Discipline aboard a 1600s English naval vessel was a delicate balance of control through fear and punishment, and an imbalance could lead to complete and total anarchy.

Sailing was closer to exploring than navigating, since there were no accurate charts or Global Positioning Systems. Nowadays, we can ascertain our arrival times with up-to-the-minute accuracy. In those days, it was much different and extremely difficult. Therefore, the length of a voyage could rarely be determined with any level of accuracy; the most anyone could do was guess. Crewmembers could become agitated if the voyage dragged on for too long without an end in sight, so food and water storage areas had to be constantly watched.[2]

Sailors were famously known to be a superstitious lot and any maritime mishap could be construed as an omen. Most captains did not have a high tolerance for these behaviors. In order to avoid any uncertainty about who

---

2. Higginson, 1899

was in charge, the captain gave his trusted officers the freedom to deal with offenses directly, swiftly, and cruelly. The most feared and dreaded form of punishment was being tied to the mast and lashed with the "cat o' nine tails", which was a nine-tipped leather strap. The severity and execution of this punishment was typically determined by the offense committed. For instance, a crewmember falling asleep on his watch warranted one of the harshest forms of this punishment. The offender was lashed openly as an example to the rest of the crew.

In light of this, most people think merchant ships must have been a better experience for a sailor. Actually, that was not really the case. The discipline was the same, the only difference being that the captain and his main officers were often the major stakeholders in the profitability of the vessel. Many times on merchant ships, the captain and officers would reduce the rations of the ordinary crew members, but not their own. From the officers' point of view, it was just good business practice. The general wellbeing of the ordinary crew members was just not a consideration. It was simply business, no matter how inhumane or cruel it seems to us now.

During the Anglo Spanish War (which lasted from 1585 to 1604) and the War of Spanish Succession (1701 to 1714), England found itself lagging behind other nations in terms of naval strength, and in an aim to ameliorate that, they increased the practice of privateering. Under this practice, England issued letters of marque (basically a government license) to private vessels which authorized them to attack the vessels of nations with whom they were at war. At the height of privateering, England was so desperate that it allowed the vessels it commissioned to keep 100% of the bounty they seized while at war. This made privateering the major catalyst for piracy.

BIMINI AND THE BLACK FLAG

Legendary pirates including Henry Morgan, William Kidd, "Calico" Jack Rackham, and even Edward "Blackbeard" Teach were born of the change to the seafaring way of life. Those who had a letter of marque and had been seizing Spanish galleons with caches of gold, silver, and jewels on behalf of their queen found themselves discarded by their mother nations. Unemployed and bitter, they began conquering ships of any nation, enslaving crew members, and looting along the way. These skilled and hardened men had no country to call home and were still covered head to toe with physical, emotional, and psychological scars from the cruel treatment of naval captains and merchant officers. Many men lost their lives in battles with other pirates. It was a continuous cycle of violence and savagery.

Eventually, in an act of self-preservation, these skilled men set up systems of checks and balances. The Articles of Agreement (or "pirate code") was a document signed and displayed aboard vessels. It set up descriptions of duties and rules for the appropriation of stolen goods, discipline for offenses, and even compensation for those who were injured in fierce battles with other pirate ships. These articles functioned as law and kept the entire population of the ship in line.

Pirates didn't like arbitrary authority, and if these crew members were going to put their lives on the line and go to war with any government, they were not going to put up with unjust or cruel treatment aboard their vessels. This led to the election of pirate captains. Pirate captains were constantly worried about keeping their jobs, so they learned it was good practice to keep the crew happy. Captains rarely had the last word about which ships to engage, or what seas to pirate. These matters were put to a vote by the crew. The one time the captain did have complete and uncontested authority was when the ship was engaged in battle.

The second in command on a pirate vessel was the quartermaster. He would distribute arms for battle, organize food rations, and was the only man authorized to hand out punishment. However, before any punishment, a general vote usually decided whether the offense was punishment-worthy. The quartermaster also oversaw the accounting and distribution of coins or other items of value. The quartermaster carried out his various duties in the open and under the watchful eye of his crew. The method of dividing spoils or booty rarely came to a dispute.

The preferred pirate vessels of the Caribbean and Bahamas were sloops. They were around sixty feet in length and carried a crew comprised of no less than 75 men with just under 20 guns. A sloop was equipped with a single mast made of a large sail area and a shallow draft, and it was capable of reaching speeds just under 12 knots when sailing in favorable conditions. Some of these sloops were even outfitted with oars to give them an added advantage in light winds when most vessels were becalmed.

The Spanish empire was successful in its conquests of Central and South America and had begun stripping those countries of riches using convoys of galleon vessels. A galleon was a large, slow multi-decked cargo ship that carried the riches from Central America and Mexico back to the motherland. Spain had control of territories reaching as far as Cuba and Hispaniola (Haiti), and these large treasure convoys had the protection of Spanish authorities when sailing by these islands. The tricky part usually came when they made the northbound turn to catch the easterly winds and the Gulf Stream current around the coast of Florida.

Pirates had made Nassau in the Bahamas their self-proclaimed capital, and Bimini was 120 nautical miles west, or at most a two- or three-day sail. Right on the doorstep of the Gulf Stream, Bimini was a perfect vantage point for a pirate looking for treasure-laden Spanish galleons or merchant ships. The freshwater spring on South Bimini made it possible for pirates to remain nourished and energetic for extended periods of time. Pirates of that era had the "home field advantage". Their knowledge of the areas they pirated gave them a huge advantage over galleons or merchant ships passing through.

When pirate crews engaged other ships, the idea was to disable the vessel and then board it, taking anything and everything of value. High-value items were mostly gemstones, precious metals, textiles, and other easily transported materials. In some cases, though, crewmembers were forced to join the pirates or were sold off into slavery.

Spanish galleon and merchant ship crews were basically simple sailors with little combat or artillery experience. They had a consistent route and smaller crews, because more men would cut into the vessels' profitability. Once a black flag was spotted on the horizon, it turned out that not too many crewmembers were willing to put their life on the line for a minuscule salary and poor treatment.

Pirates knew their crews' and their vessels' capabilities in every imaginable condition. Once a prize vessel was disabled, usually by disabling the rudder or using chain shot, the pirates would use grappling hooks and secure the maimed vessel to their own. Now came the most dangerous part: the boarding. Victimized vessels usually had a small complement of arms and their only hope was to defeat the pirate crew and hopefully steal their vessel. This rarely happened. Pirates were heavily armed and dressed in such a way that their mere appearance struck fear into the hearts of their victims. Blackbeard, the most famous pirate of all time, was rumored to put gunpowder in the braids of his hair and set it on fire as a shock-and-awe technique.

Imagine a poor young sailor who was treated harshly by his captain staring at a pirate crew brandishing their weapons. For joining them, he's promised booty worth double what he would make in his lifetime if he weren't about to lose his life. Not a difficult decision to make.

After the boarding process was over, there was usually an informal trial for the vessel's captain. In the incredibly rare circumstance he was found not guilty, the captain got to keep his ship, some cargo, and most importantly, his life. A guilty captain usually watched his ship get demolished and was likely interrogated about other ships passing along the same route. Any crew members who weren't asked or who refused to join the pirates were marooned, killed, or sold off into slavery.

As the mid 1700s approached, both merchants and empires were losing ships regularly, and governments were under pressure by their wealthy aristocratic citizens to facilitate safe and secure trade on the high seas. In 1718, England sent a naval fleet under the command of Woods Rogers on a mission with the authority to pardon all pirates under the condition they no longer engage in piracy. Those who didn't accept the condition would be hung.

Many tired, older pirates took the offer, including the so-called "pirate president" Benjamin Horningold, while others like Charles Vane made a daring escape. When Vane received word Rogers' arrival in Nassau, he set fire to a French ship he had recently captured, right in front of Rogers' flagship. Vane even dared to fire a few shots before making his escape. It is rumored that Vane and Blackbeard thought the English were no match for them and that they could eventually take the island back. However, Blackbeard would die later that year.

Rogers' arrival enhanced England's presence in the Bahamas, and their Admiralty vessels served as judge, jury, and executioner for pirates in the area. Bounties were collected and coastal harbors were decorated with the bodies of pirates rotting in gibbets. By the time Blackbeard's head was hanging from George Maynard's bowsprit, power was slowly seeping away from the pirates and back into the grasp of sovereign authorities.

Though England now had control over Nassau and the Bahamas, the American experiment was already beginning. The Bahamas and the New Colonies were often viewed as a drain on the finances of their parent governments. The locals that were put in charge began to harbor resentment and started to think, "Why send the profits home and not keep them for us?" The piratical passion for democracy was beginning to spread from the seas to this new world called America.

PIRATE FACT AND FICTION

There have been quite a lot of myths that surround the pirate legacy and I can assure you that it's probably because they wanted it that way. The pirate life has certainly been romanticized in books and movies. One thing that is certain is that piracy certainly wasn't a dull life. While Hollywood might have missed a lot of it, the hardness and excitement of the pirate life was definitely a spectacle.

Did pirates have nicknames?

Yes, but "alias" might be a more accurate term. You rarely hear about successful pirates, because they went by several names. That helped them avoid criminal prosecution, and helped them protect their families. Muliple aliases also made sure that if they ever decided to quit the pirate life, they could live leisurely in anonymity and it would be difficult for authorities to track them through their birth information.

Did pirates make prisoners walk the plank?

There is no documented evidence that adequately supports this fact, but each crew of pirates had their own code and established set of rules they lived by. Because piracy was done for profit, most prisoners were sold into slavery immediately after being captured. Crew members usually warranted a trial to determine their guilt or innocence and marooning was their more common punishment.

Did pirates bury their treasure?

Pirates were excellent mariners but terrible business men. Their money mainly went to boozing, carousing with women, and other vices. There are a couple of well-documented stories about pirates burying their treasure.

One of them is privateer-turned-pirate William Kidd. He learned that he was to be hanged and immediately buried his treasure in hopes of buying his freedom with his loot. The treasure was never found and many large efforts are launched from time to time in hopes of finding it.

Did women ever become pirates?

There were not many known women pirates, possibly because the largely superstitious pirates believed it was bad luck to have women onboard a boat. However, a few women were able to conceal their sexuality from other crew members. Anne Bonny and Mary Read are two of the most famous female pirates. Some people say that the most successful pirate was Mrs. Cheng, a woman who once presided over a confederation of some 50,000 pirates!

Did pirates have a code?

Yes, they did. The pirate code was a set of rules that varied in concept and composition from one crew to the next. They were usually voted on democratically among crew members and they defined the method of division of stolen goods, the rules of discipline, punishment for offenses, and compensation for injuries. They were the visionaries in democracy!

What is the difference between pirate and privateer?

Privateers were mercenaries on privately-owned boats who were under direct orders from a government to attack ships. Pirates did not take orders from a specific government; they attacked ships as voted by the crew.

What is a Buccaneer?

Long before they were a football team, these were ordinary European settlers in the Caribbean, predominantly the West Indies and Haiti. They made their living by selling smoked meat from wild cattle and boar to passing ships. They were also famously known for attacking and harassing Spanish ships.

Did pirates have peg legs and hooks and did they wear eye patches?

They probably did but the whole thing has been greatly exaggerated by movies and novelists. These guys worked hard and drank even harder and there was no OSHA around to see that things were done safely. Back then, they were not overly interested in methods; all that mattered was getting the right results. Limbs were often lost in battle or on the job. The eye patch may have been common -- some believe it gave them an advantage by keeping one eye adjusted for bright sunlight above deck and the other for dark conditions below deck.

Were pirates blood thirsty thieves?

Pirates typically only fought as hard as they had to, but sometimes that meant until death. Since their sole purpose was profit, it made no sense to destroy a vessel with cargo that could later be sold. A typical tactic was to fly the same country's flag as the vessel they were targeting. When they were close enough, they would hoist their jolly roger and the prize vessel would usually see no way out and surrender. Other times, all out battles ensued, with the victor taking all the spoils.

Did pirates use treasure maps?

Not a single pirate treasure map has ever been found in history. That isn't to say they're not out there, though!

Chapter 2

AMERICA AND THE BAHAMAS

*I*n 1775, America was at war with England and colonists that were loyal to the crown tried desperately to foil the rebel colonists' plots. Lord Dunmore, a loyal English governor of the colony of Virginia, had ordered British troops to take ammunition and supplies to Nassau. Montfort Browne, the Bahamian governor, received word that colonist rebels may attempt to seize the powder and ammunitions.

In early February 1776, the newly-assembled U.S. Navy was very small and was comprised of mainly citizens, not soldiers. They set out on a mission to seize desperately needed supplies. They faced gale force winds for about two days, and lost two vessels due to high winds. They reached Nassau by nightfall on March 3rd but decided to hold off on any action until daybreak. This proved to be a fatal error, since their ships were spotted at daybreak, and the alarm triggered an immediate retaliation from Bahamian loyalists.

Browne ordered four guns to be fired from Fort Nassau. The fort was in a poor state from disuse, and two of the four guns came off their mounts immediately. Meanwhile, the rebel colonists heard the gunshots and realized that they had lost the element of surprise. The rebel contingent regrouped and decided to brutally ransack Fort Montague. They met no resistance.

That night, Browne was able to get a good portion of the islands' gunpowder and food supplies sent on a fast vessel to St. Augustine under the cover of darkness. Meanwhile, the colonists, after drinking most of the governor's liquor, left Nassau with just under 40 barrels of gunpowder. Governor Browne was taken hostage and later exchanged for United States General William Alexander.

The war for America's independence went on until 1783 when the financial strain had taken its toll on the royal government. Loyalists were extremely bitter and in many cases, they had their property and funds seized by the new American government.

The Bahamian population exploded with British loyalist refugees, who were almost instantly at odds with the established residents (at the time, known as "conchs"). The refugees felt that they had no representation in the government and protested openly, even rioting in some cases. It was a grueling and difficult life for these new settlers in the Bahamas. They were accustomed to an agricultural economy and tried desperately to grow cotton. The soil quickly became depleted. The loyalists and others, through many hardships, were beginning to realize that the Bahamas was not meant to be an agricultural nation. They were, however, beginning to flourish as a maritime center and they were about to receive a major economic boost from a neighboring nation.

America's economy was agriculture based and they made their money largely on the backs of slaves. The trans-Atlantic slave trade maintained the flow of cheap labor but was symbolically banned by the crown in 1807, and then banished in all English territories by 1837. All slave property was free in the Bahamas. Illegal slave traders still passed through the Bahamas and the Royal Navy was dispatched to suppress them. Slave trade vessels caught traveling through the Bahamas were immediately ordered to Nassau and most of the slave cargo was set free. England realized that the best way to suppress the trade was through naval blockades at the ports where slave traders received their cargo, and by doing so they severed a large part of the economic lifeline to the Bahamas.

That economic boost was because of America's Civil War. In 1860, Abraham Lincoln was elected President of the United States and by 1861, America was in a civil war. One of the first things the North did was to order a naval blockade of southern ports. This led to blockade running, which gave the Bahamas an economic boost.

The early phase of blockade running was to get ammunitions and goods through the blocked southern ports with wooden schooners and sloops. This dangerous and exciting way to make a living was not a difficult life for Bahamians to adapt to, given their piratical history. These blockade runners would sail ammunitions as far north as the Carolinas and south as far as Louisiana, while trying to avoid being spotted and turned over to the Union Navy.

In 1862, the Confederates' desperation for supplies increased and they focused on sidewheel steam power as a way to get their shipments through the blockades. These steam vessels were incredibly fast, stealthy, and useful in any wind direction (something that still eluded the ships of the Union Navy). The success rate of blockade running vessels had been a dismal 57.4%, but the sidewheel steamer brought the success rate for supply runs up into 80%.[3]

Economically speaking, Nassau's growth skyrocketed. Hotels, brothels, gambling houses, and bars to entertain would-be sailors sprang up seemingly overnight and gave blockade runners a place to blow off steam before running the gauntlet back to the U.S.

By 1864, the Union naval fleet had grown not only in size but also in speed and finesse. At this point in the war, it was estimated that only one of three blockade runners made it through. More than 1,000 blockade runners were captured and around 300 were destroyed. As the Civil War ended in 1865, another wave of war-weary immigrants made their way to Bimini and settled there.

---

3. Finkelman, 2009

The settlers came primarily to engage in the wrecking trade.[4] Wrecking was a huge staple of the Bahamian economy and the residents of Bimini, as, just like the pirates before them, they found themselves in a perfect position to watch vessels meet a dire fate on their doorstep. Wreckers usually received 40-60% of the salvaged goods' value and the government took the rest. Goods and profits often stayed in Bimini. At its peak, the wrecking industry employed just under 3,000 men and 300 boats out of a population of around 25,000. The total revenue brought in at its peak was £154,000 in the year 1870.

---

4. Essential Civil War Curriculum, n.d.

Chapter 3
THE LIGHTHOUSES

*T*he Imperial Lighthouse Service (ILS) of England began its construction on eleven lighthouses in the Bahamas. Three of the lighthouses were in the Bimini chain, on Gun Cay, Great Isaacs, and Cay Sal. The building of these lighthouses came with its own share of challenges and problems. Those involved in the wrecking trade went to great lengths to sabotage the lighthouse construction and to stop completion by whatever means necessary. During the construction period, several attacks were made on construction sites and walls were pulled to the ground.

In May 1836, Gun Cay became the first ILS lighthouse to be completed in the Bahamas. It was located 10 miles South of Bimini, marking the beginning of the western edge of the Bahamas. The lighthouse was made completely from stones quarried from the island and it stood 77 feet tall, painted red on the top and white on the bottom. Because it wasn't fully functional, the lighthouse was eventually reclassified as a local light and its operation and maintenance was delegated to the locals of Bimini.

The Gun Cay light was constantly in a state of disrepair, since most people felt its operation cut into the wrecking profits of the locals. In 1870, the Governor of the Bahamas received a letter from the ILS deputy inspector stating that the light was observed to be operating at a revolution rate of 30 seconds instead of the officially listed and recognized 90 seconds. This variation, though it may seem small, was actually a huge difference. This meant the light could be mistaken for any other light at Craysfoot reef that was signaling vessels to keep east and that ships might run aground due to the confusion.

With frequently changing shipping routes, the light gradually lost its importance. In May 1937, exactly one hundred years after it began operating, the Gun Cay light was extinguished for the very last time. The lantern was removed and eventually transferred to Hope Town, Abaco, and in its place, a metal tripod equipped with an automated light was erected on top of the Gun Cay lighthouse. The lighthouse still stands today, although the interior part of it is dilapidated and off limits. However, it still makes for a fantastic photo opportunity for cruisers sailing around the general area.

Gun Cay Lighthouse
(photo credit: David Miller)

The second ILS lighthouse in the Bimini area was the Cay Sal lighthouse, erected in 1839. It is the southernmost lighthouse in the Bimini island chain and it stands 70 feet tall. It marks the southern entrance to the Florida Straits. It was a widely used light and was fully operational for just nearly 100 years. As the maritime world was abandoning sails for steam, quicker routes were being discovered and used. The Cay Sal light was extinguished for the last time on January 9, 1934, and the site was completely abandoned by its keepers on March 4th of that year.

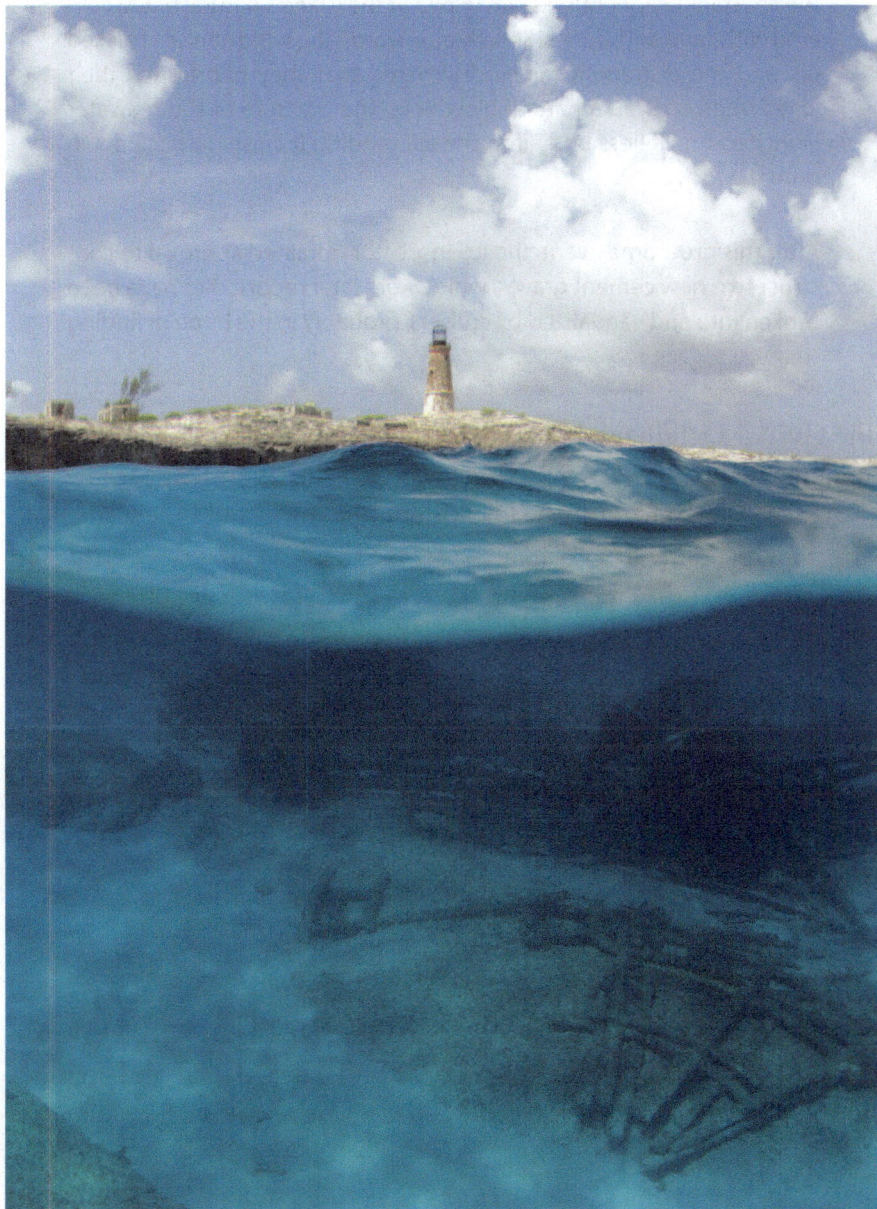

Cay Sal Lighthouse with Paddle Wheel wreck

Legend Has It

A macabre story has been attributed to the Cay Sal lighthouse site. It is said that in the early days of its service the main light keeper died. Because the ground is coral rock, no grave could be dug, so his family and the assistant keeper buried him in one of the island's natural holes, covered with sand and stones. Shortly afterwards, the wind and seas picked up, and the distraught family discovered that they had buried their loved one's body in a natural blow hole. The pressure of the seawater launched the lifeless body into the air, sending it crashing back down onto the rocks.[5]

After this gruesome event, the ILS inspector obtained approval to construct two new cement graves, which were later reported to have been broken into and vandalized by cruisers, probably in the hope of finding treasure.

The Cay Sal Lighthouse has been steadily decaying into a haunting, eerie monument over the years since its closure. During World War II, the U.S. Coast Guard put an automated beacon on the tower and built a small airstrip for small aircraft and fighter planes. The beacon and air strip were abandoned after the end of the war, but in the following decades were used illegally by drug smugglers shipping cocaine from Colombia. In the 1970s, a small Bahamian defense force of four men was stationed on the island to thwart drug smuggling. The creative way they halted drug trade through the area was by blowing huge holes in the runway and making it unusable. The lighthouse structure is still there today and is a spot where Cuban refugees often wash up seeking temporary asylum from Cuba. Don't be surprised if you see the U.S. Coast Guard patrolling the area.

The last of the lighthouses to be established in Bimini was the Great Isaacs light. It is about 19 miles north of Bimini and has been the focal point of legends over the years. The light first lit the area on August 1, 1859, demarcating of the northern point of Bimini. Great Isaacs is a small and uninhabited cay, just under a mile long and 300 feet across at its widest point.

---

5.   Coker, 2009.

Legend Has It

One of Great Issacs' legends is that of the wicked hurricane passed through a few years before the lighthouse was constructed. The force of the storm sunk many vessels in the area. When the storm was over, a party of fishermen who were near the cay on a moonlit night spotted a large white animal roaming the shore and decided to investigate. At the place where the lighthouse now stands, they were horrified to see the corpse of a large white horse floating among the debris and many dead bodies from a recent wreck. Surprisingly, one of the corpses was a woman clutching an infant in her arms – and he was still alive! After being treated for minor injuries, the boy was adopted by a family leaving for England. The legend is still circulated today, and, up until 1913, many keepers of this station reported that on every full moon the "grey woman" was seen wandering the shore, looking for her lost child.

The Great Issacs lighthouse still stands today, and although the keepers' houses are quite decrepit, the buildings make for wonderful photos for people sailing by.

Great Issac's Lighthouse

Chapter 4
THE RUMRUNNERS

*I*n 1919, the United States Congress signed the Volstead Act, better known as Prohibition, which outlawed the sale and consumption of liquor and alcohol within the borders of the country. Bimini, just 45 nautical miles from the coast of Miami, found itself a prime location for rumrunners to make quick and easy money. Just a few generations after the golden age of piracy and only one generation after blockade running, it was not difficult for Bimini to once again fully embrace their outlaw heritage. Of course, from the Bahamian standpoint, they were really doing nothing wrong; it was simple economics at work. Money poured in just as fast as the rum casks could be filled.

Bruce Bethel was Bimini's most notorious rumrunner. He was an Englishman who lost his arm fighting during World War I. After the war, he settled in Nassau, where he and his brother opened a liquor store. As one of the only liquor stores that offered free samples, the business thrived. After prohibition began in the United States, Bethel, being a sharp businessman, decided to expand his business. He chose Bimini as the site of his new liquor warehouse because of its close proximity to Florida. Within a few years of his arrival in Bimini, his fortune afforded him great status among the British subjects, rivaling even the island commissioner.

Bethel built a makeshift dock out of naturally-occurring mangrove roots, leading to one of his heavily-padlocked warehouses. He welcomed smugglers to temporarily store their supplies with him; for each case of liquor, which the smugglers would sell in the States for around $100, Bethel made about $20. The incredible success of his business operation was well-known across the islands, and many black residents of Bimini went to work for him in the hopes of making a decent wage that was enough to feed their families. Bethel also had the Bimini Rod and Gun Club built as a way of improving tourism.

Along with warehouses and hotels, Bethel also purchased the *Sapona*, one of 17 concrete liberty ships designed and made for WWI. The Sapona had not seen any wartime action, and before it landed in Bethel's hands it was owned by Carl Fisher, a prominent Miami resident and founder of the Indy 500. The wreck of the *Sapona* can still be seen today, hauntingly facing the islands as if trying to say, "I'm still here," despite Mother Nature and all her elements. It was purchased in Miami and brought to Bimini where Bethel used it as a liquor transport and storage location.

Bethel and the *Sapona* were near the Gun Cay area when the storm which would become known as the "Great Miami Hurricane" hit. Winds of 150 miles per hour and massive seas raged while Bethel tried to get the *Sapona* and her stock to the safety of Bimini. The seas picked the *Sapona* up and cruelly set her on top of the wreck of a Spanish galleon. The collision split the stern from the hull, and sent Bethel's liquor down into the deep.

Bethel never recovered financially from this disaster, and reportedly began to lose his grip on his sanity[6]. While in the process of turning the *Sapona*'s remains into a nightclub, he was swept out to sea, last seen clinging with his only arm to a piece of detached wood. The man who had survived World War I with debilitating injuries and amassed a fortune, was swallowed up by the sea, penniless, in 1950.

The rum-running days were some of the most prosperous in the history of Bimini. New businesses were popping up, including the famed Compleat Angler Hotel, built by Helen Duncombe, the former island commissioner's

---

6.   Power & Motoryacht, n.d.

widow, and her two daughters. Constructed with the wood from old barges and barrels, this must have been a massive undertaking and it speaks volumes about the level of determination these early women of Bimini had. The Angler, as it was often called, was one of Bimini's most frequented hotels and bars. Hosting many prominent people over the years, its most famous guest was writer Ernest Hemingway. The Angler was one of his favorite haunts while he was working on his novels or partaking in one his favorite pastimes: big game fishing.

Before being destroyed by a fire in 2006, the Angler was operated by the Brown family as a bar, hotel, and an antique museum. The fire was devastating to the community, which lost two treasures; the historic Angler and all its vintage Hemingway-era photos, and owner Julian Brown, a decorated 1969 track and field Olympian. If you visit the site of the Compleat Angler today, only the stone fireplace still stands, as a grave reminder of what once surrounded it.

HEMINGWAY AND BIG GAME FISHING

Ernest Hemingway, the Pulitzer and Nobel prize-winning writer, lived a life of indulgence. He is almost personally responsible for the rise of sport fishing and was one of the International Game Fishing Association's charter members. From the late 1920s until his death in 1961 he was a frequent visitor of Bimini, where he would drink, fish, eat, sleep, and drink some more. Nearly every bar in Bimini claims that he was a frequent patron.

Hemingway was an accomplished fisherman who loved the thrill of the fight. From his legendary fishing boat *Pilar*, he would spend hours landing 500-pound tuna and 1,000-pound marlins. He was instrumental in helping design rods, reels, and even the way fishing vessels were rigged. Hooking a fish was the easy part. The hard part was landing the fish without it being mutilated by sharks. Hemingway, or "Papa" as the natives refer to him, was famous for tommy-gunning mako sharks that would try to make an easy meal out of his trophy. He was the first fisherman to land an unmutilated marlin. The rod he used for this feat was a "Bimini King", made by Tycoon Tackle, which sold for $150 – equivalent to $2,000 in today's currency!

Legend Has It

We know the competition was fierce among anglers. According to famous Bimini banjo player Nathaniel "Piccolo Pete" Saunders, the legendary fight between Ernest Hemingway and *Collier's* publisher Joseph Knapp was the talk of the islands. There are several versions of this story, but the most consistent version starts with Mr. Knapp trying to enter a mutilated marlin for a record. Hemingway confronted him with the rule that no mutilated fish could be entered for a record. It's unclear if Knapp didn't recognize Hemingway or just didn't care who he was, but he reportedly said something along the lines of "Go to hell you big fat slob," and Hemingway gave him a haymaker right there on the dock.

Piccolo Pete would compose a song called *The Big Fat Slob of Bimini*, still sung by some of the old timers today. The song was recorded on Victory Records and is sold on CD in many of the island gift shops.

Long after Hemingway's death, Bimini remains a top sport fishing destination. Excited anglers make pilgrimages from all corners of the world to have a dance with the legendary marlins or seek a more even-tempered marine adversary like a bonefish.

Bonefishing is extremely popular on Bimini today, with a host of guides willing to take you through the mangroves. Martin Luther King, Jr. was guided by bonefishing boat-building legend Ansil Saunders. Legend has it he took King to Bimini's Healing Hole so he could compose his Nobel prize acceptance speech *I've Been to the Mountain Top*.[7]

If you are looking for a thrill, you haven't lived until you've seen a defiant marlin at the other end of your line, fighting with every ounce of its might. You harness yourself into the fighting chair and start cranking. As you start to gain line, the marlin strips it away, then you gain some more, then it takes some more. This can go on for hours and it's as much a mental battle as a physical one, because that beast isn't going to give up and neither are you. You hope the line and the rod hold. After you boat that fish, the sting in

---

7.   "Martin Luther King, Jr. Pilgrimage", n.d.

your wrists and arms will remind you for the next two weeks of how hard you fought, and you will remember that experience for the rest of your life!

THE HOOLIGAN NAVY

In 1942, the United States found itself in the middle of an all-out war with the combined nations of Japan and Germany. If England ruled the seas with its navy, then Germany was the undisputed ruler of the underwater world with a fleet of 64 U-boats capable of sinking up to 130 vessels and well over half a million tons of allied shipping cargo in the Bahamas.

As the U.S. was caught off guard, its navy was ill equipped, and President Roosevelt commissioned non-military merchant ships, quickly outfitting them with meager amounts of low-quality guns, ammunition, and explosives.

Papa Hemingway, never one to shy away from a fight or an adventure, commissioned his famed 38-foot fishing vessel *Pilar* to go hunt and gun down German U-boats, becoming a member of the "Hooligan Navy." Hemingway's plan was to sneak up on an unsuspecting U-boat, open its hatch, and lodge grenades deep down inside its shaft and cargo. However, when submarines surfaced, they diligently watched for enemy boats, especially in hostile territories. Hemingway never confirmed a U-boat sighting. Some speculate he saw the war effort as just another adventure with his friends.

I'm not sure if America knew how close the war actually was to the United States mainland. U-boats routinely patrolled the territorial waters of the U.S. and the Bahamas. U-506, under the command of Erich Wurdemann, opened up a rampage of destruction and desolation on the shipping traffic from Bimini to the Cay Sal Bank. The main cause for the anger that drove this violent campaign was the insistence of the United States that channel markers and coastal city lights should not be blacked out -- as if there were no war going on at all for the citizens of the United States.

It took about six months to a year of this before the United States' six vessels were torpedoed and fully sunk by U-boats in the Straits of Florida.

Legend Has It

There are many stories of sunken U-boats within the recreational dive limits that are all over the Bahamas. Perhaps the most famous is the Gun Cut U-boat. The story that has been passed down through various island characters over the years is that there was a sunken boat on the west side of Gun Cay; a distance that measures just less than a quarter mile. It is what some would consider a pile of junk pieces of hull. I personally do not think this a U-boat; there is a good possibility that it is merely scattered wreckage from the Alma B, an inter-island mail boat that capsized between Gun and North Cat Cay. The Alma B is still on the ocean floor, upside down and strongly buried in the ocean sand.

Boats leaving Florida and which were silhouetted against the bright lights of Florida's coastal cities were like shooting ducks in a barrel for a U-boat captain. They United States and all allied naval forces increasingly stepped up their presence in the territorial waters of the United States and refueling and supplies proved to be increasingly difficult and eventually, they were completely driven out of the area (or at least, so we think). The British forces captured the U-570 and confiscated the German's Enigma code deciphering machine. It took a while for the code to be cracked but with it and RDF (Radio Directional Finder) technology which could key in on which direction the radio signal was coming from when German U-boats would surface for radio communication vessels and aircraft. This was a huge improvement from the Hooligan Navy's half drunk crews wildly scanning the horizon for any sights and clues of the presence of the enemy.

If any German subs were sunk in the Bimini area, it is highly likely that it was in deep water and once the vessel was disabled, it was taken far North from the point of the impact by the North bound gulfstream current. So if there are any sunken U-boats in the Bimini area, they are more than likely buried in very deep and strong water. After the end of World War II, Bimini coasted slowly in terms of her economy by relying on the contribution of aspects such as tourism and big game fishing. Bimini was about to get a major shot in the arm economically, once again relying on those outlaw roots and again turning to the sea.

Chapter 5
MIAMI VICE

*O*nce prohibition ended, Bimini fell into an economic hangover. In 1973, after a hard effort, the Bahamas gained its independence from England and became its own nation. Bimini was doing what it did best to get by: a little tourism and subsistence fishing. During the late 1970s and early 1980s, the Bahamas stripped Cuba of its fishing rights to their waters. Once again, the area's market was flooded with boat captains and vessels that had no feasible way of making money. These captains knew the waters and inlets of Florida better than anyone else, so they once again turned to their ancestors for inspiration. The commercial fishing void quickly filled with running large amounts of cocaine and marijuana, as demand for drugs increased in the United States. During the "Miami Vice" period, Bahamian Attorney General Paul Adderley said of the U.S. "We inherit your vices."[8]

The smugglers would get the product supply from South American drug lords and cartels by plane at prearranged drop points throughout the Bahamas. The smugglers were ingenious in bypassing authority protocols through creative techniques. They filled blenders with water and cocaine, then put the solutions in insect sprayers and sprayed down every inch of decoy boats so boarding drug dogs would get hits on everything. This frustrated DEA agents to no end. Smugglers also had boats designed by actual racing boat builders outfitted with the latest electronics, including night

8.   Allen, 1988

vision and radar detection. One U.S. Customs agent reported being circled by a defiant, cocky smuggler. The smuggler made off in a much faster boat while screaming obscenities and waving his middle finger, leaving the Customs agent unable to do anything but watch him escape.[9]

It is reported that as many as five boats, some with product and some without, would leave Bimini every night around 9 p.m. They set out, screaming towards Miami, playing a hair-raising shell game with authorities. The smugglers also had lookouts stationed in boats at various inlets. If they saw the authorities they would go as far as setting fires and making other distress calls to draw the authorities' resources away from where the smugglers needed to be.

Once the smugglers made it across the Gulf Stream, they would navigate through the mangroves of the Florida Keys, or pull right up to docks in downtown Miami and offload their goods into vans. Then they would immediately go off into the night. For a long time, these smugglers were seemingly phantoms; nobody saw them or knew for sure how they operated. If one of these boats happened to realize that they were being tailed, they would off-load the drugs right into the water. The bales – yes, literally bales – of pot and cocaine would wash up in Bimini so often that they called them "square groupers". Older custom officials say these bales were chalked up as a loss, and whoever found them would turn around and sell it for whatever price they wished. Due to the popularity and great demand for drugs at that time, these sales would inevitably yield quick, outrageous profits. At its peak, the drug smuggling trade was an industry that was worth more than $110 billion. With sums of money like that in play, turf wars were a natural side effect.

The first overt shot fired in the cocaine wars was the Dadeland Mall Massacre in Miami, Florida on July 11, 1979. A hit was ordered by Griselda Blanco, a boss for the famed Pablo Escobar's drug cartel network, which was run like a multinational corporation. Two men in a nondescript van with the logo "Happy Time Party Supply" on it ambushed two men in a Mercedes in broad daylight. Jumping out of the van with machine guns,

---

9.   Cummings, 1970

they sprayed hundreds of 9 mm and 45-caliber rounds until the men in the Mercedes lay dead. Shoppers were understandably terrified.

Police were overwhelmed, and some suspect they were accepting bribes.[10] It was hard for law enforcement to get a grasp of how the cartels were working due to the influx of Spanish-speaking Cuban refugees and Columbian cartel members who rarely carried identification. The glut of bodies turning up in Miami, between Cuban refugee traffickers and Colombian cartel suppliers, was astounding. Law enforcement didn't know what role the person played in cartel operations, and it took the better part of the decade to grasp the hierarchy of both the supply and traffic operations. This era earned Miami, a city where the economy was largely driven by tourism, one of the deadliest reputations of all American cities.[11]

It's not that hard to see how a young man or a struggling boat captain could easily get lured into the drug-smuggling lifestyle. If you made the run, you could be compensated with hundreds of thousands of dollars. Like most drugs and illegal business ventures, however, this lifestyle was short-lived. It got bloody very quickly, and older smugglers with families who got caught often turned states' evidence for the DEA. Waves of paranoia rapidly began to take over the cartels and in turn, they vented their anger by ruthlessly taking vengeance on the smugglers. Bodies were turning up in the Miami River a couple times each week, and there were massive public shootouts between warring drug factions.

These overt public blood baths were obviously detrimental to both Bimini's and Miami's economies, as they both relied heavily on their public image to bring in tourism money. With a joint effort by the Bahamian defense force and the U.S. Coast Guard, the drug trade has diminished considerably. The glamour and adventure may have lured the smugglers into the outlaw trade, but by the late 1990s, the party began to wind down. The cartels had been ruthless in establishing their dominance on the area, but the Bahamian and United States' officials were equally ruthless with harsh punishments and prison sentences for smugglers. With an outright war

---

10.   Nordheimer, 1986
11.   Meek, 2012

declared on drugs by the U.S. government and Bahamian law enforcement authorities, it left the smugglers with little choice. When the party was over, most of the smugglers had either been killed or imprisoned.

THE LIVEABOARD INDUSTRY

Despite the blight of drug trafficking, the 1980s and 1990s brought new, legal business to Bimini with the recreational dive industry. Kids that grew up watching Jacques Cousteau documentaries and the classic Lloyd Bridges series *Sea Hunt* were now dive shop owners looking for exotic destinations, and what could be more perfect than a tiny, unspoiled island just 45 nautical miles from Miami?

Bimini was host to several live boards beginning in the 1980s: most notably Sea Fever and the famed Blackbeard's Cruises. These vessels would depart typically on Saturdays and make their way towards Bimini, arriving late Saturday or early Sunday morning. The captains would then clear customs and the birth of an industry was born.

I got my start as a captain in 2001, relocating to the tropics from the cold, gray Michigan winter. I'll never forget (and I don't think any crewmember ever will forget) my arrival to the boat. She was in port on a maintenance week and I thought arriving after 5 p.m. would be well after working hours. I can't tell you how astonished I was to find them all still working. After introducing myself to the captain, she said "Nice to meet you . . . pick up a grinder." The saying is "you have to pay your dues before you sing the blues." There is certainly an element of hazing for new crew members.

I learned very quickly that each different captain ran his or her boat their specific way and that the upper management backed these captains. The crews between the three vessels in our fleet were definitely rivals amongst each other, but also part of a very unique fraternity and family.

The hours we worked were subject to change and the mood of the crew was largely dependent on Mother Nature. Under optimal conditions, most vessels could make it across the Gulf Stream to Bimini in six hours. That was typical except for the months of November through April. The winter cold fronts bring blistering northeast winds that push against the Gulf Stream's mighty three knots making the seas stand up and build.

The live aboard dive industry out of Florida to Bimini gave scuba divers a bold slap of adventure almost from departure. The Gulf Stream takes with the same hand it gives with. At one moment it can be as calm as a lake but if Mother Nature is angry at Neptune, the ocean will rage like something out of the worst pages of *Revelation*. I have sailed in many parts of the world but some of the most terrifying moments I have experienced have been in the Gulf Stream.

During my second week with the company, the crossing to the Bahamas was very nice. Just one week later, we crossed back on the cusp of Hurricane Michelle. I couldn't believe we actually crossed as the weather forecast called for 20-foot seas!

To this day, Mother Nature continues to surprise me. Another phenomenon I didn't expect with the live-aboard life is how you board a boat with strangers and become lifelong friends by the end of the week. It doesn't matter who you are (or who you think you are), the old saying "We're all in the same boat" holds true. We'll be drinking from the same water tank, using the same head (that's what sailors call the bathroom), and living the same dream.

Just like the pirates that roamed the water three hundred years before us, we are a vessel searching out our own prize – no, not a sail on the horizon, but what is under that horizon. And what a treasure it is to seek -- that majestic, epic, underwater moment that humbles us and reminds us exactly where we are in the grand scheme of nature.

The vast majority of my crossings have been amazingly calm and wonderful escapes from the stateside craziness. There is no other sense and true embodiment of freedom and camaraderie like being on a boat.

Nowadays, the live aboard dive industry from Miami to Bimini is able to offer pristine scuba diving at an affordable price. The crew's number one job is to facilitate your ultimate dive vacation. These hardworking, multitasking mariners are some of the most professional on the water. They handle everything right on the vessel, from dishwashing to air conditioning repair, and are drug tested regularly. The crews are an integral part of their local economy.

There are still a few old timers around who worked on the boats in the early days, which they call the "Pre-Critique Era." They love to tell outrageous (but probably true) stories that always start out with "Before critiques . . ." then launch into a yarn about finding a square grouper and getting shot at by drug runners. Rumor has it that one captain posted a memo banning crew members from doing cocaine on the main salon table.

These boats would usually tie up to Weech's Dock in Bimini, and watch a Chalks float plane land or take off on their way in. Saralee Pinder or Sherry at the famous End of the World Saloon would wave to the boats as they came in, signaling guests to the saloon for drinks. After dark, Alice Town was filled with a hundred or so rum-filled scuba divers staggering back and forth between the bars thumping their chests, chasing girls, and bragging about their spearfishing harvest – "living the dream."

Chapter 6

PRESENT DAY BIMINI

From the late 1990s to the early 2000s, several infrastructure and developmental projects began on North and South Bimini islands, and there are now two large resorts on each island. The Resort World Bimini, with Hilton hotel and casino, is located on the North Island on beautiful, serene Paradise Point, and is accessible by boat. On the South Island, in a less-populated area is the Bimini Sands resort, which offers secluded beachfront accommodations and awesome scuba diving spots. The channel that was dredged between the two islands accommodates vessels up to 180 feet, and there are 94 slips. The resorts are the main source of economic development today, but the island has not lost its small-town charm. Bimini is still a small community where everyone seems to know everyone else, and there is a strong sense of enduring faith.

Radio Beach is lined with several shacks that serve ice cold drinks and authentic local dishes. Bimini's proximity to the Gulf Stream usually brings in fresh fish year-round and trying their renown conch salad is a must. In the late afternoon or early evening you can catch the fisherman coming in and tying up to the docks and purchase some fresh fish or lobster if it is in season. Most of the marina hotels have grills, so you can either grill your purchase yourself or take it to one of the shacks on Radio Beach—just remember to tip kindly.

Bimini lures in visitors from all over from the world with the siren song of their mythic lore, and their proximity to Florida makes this seven-mile-long island the perfect relaxation spot and holiday escape. Bimini's aqua waters will have you relaxing and resetting your internal clock to "island time." You can explore its trails, kayak through the mangroves, or even channel your inner Hemingway and give big game fishing a go.

There is no doubt that the island has gone through many changes; it has truly experienced peaks and valleys over the years. Bimini is always pushing forward while staying rooted into their colorful past. However, there is one part of the island that has remained consistent over the centuries, and that part is the DIVING!

Chapter 7
MARINE LIFE

*B*imini is comprised of some of the finest and most exquisite diving areas I have ever seen throughout the span of my career. The tidal flow of Bimini and its general proximity to the Gulf Stream brings in nutrients, maintaining the purity and visibility of the water and reef systems. The Bimini islands are also home to some of the healthiest reefs I've ever laid eyes on. The site diversity has everything from wrecks and reefs to awe-inspiring walls, all excellent sites to visit for both research and leisure purposes.

One way to enhance your scuba experience is through participating in an organized shark feed. Bimini is one of only two places in the entire world where you can see one of the most elusive creatures that live in the ocean: the Great Hammerhead. People from all walks of life travel from all over the world to take part in this surprisingly safe experience!

Just remember: the safety measures put in place for scuba divers only work if you use them. **Plan your dive, and dive your plan.** Bimini is a remote island and help is usually hours away.

SPEAR FISHING

First, some rules and restrictions: In the Bahamas, you are not allowed to use scuba gear or an air compressor to harvest fish, conch, crawfish, or other marine animals. A Hawaiian sling is the only legal and approved spearfishing device in the Bahamas. Also, spearfishing is not allowed within one mile of the coast of New Providence, within one mile of the south coast of Freeport, Grand Bahama, and within 200 yards of the coast of all the outer islands, including (and especially) Bimini. Spearing or taking marine animals by any other means is strictly prohibited within national sea parks; all crimes of this nature are punishable by law. There are numerous Lionfish Derbies hosted throughout the Bahamas which help in the eradication of these invasive predators. Spearfishing restrictions also apply to the indiscriminate and unapproved taking of Lionfish when not participating in events sanctioned and approved by the government. In these events, or for tourism or research purposes, a waiver of the spearfishing regulations is granted for a specific period of time, after which the waiver becomes invalid.

LIONFISH

Lionfish are native to the Indian Pacific waters, and exactly how they got into Bahamian waters is still a major topic of debate. They are an invasive species and have done a lot of damage to fish life on reefs. They are out-eating, out-breeding, and outliving indigenous fish. A lionfish has no natural predators in the Bahamas and is capable of reproducing quickly in almost any environment -- a female is capable of spawning two million eggs per year, and lionfish can spawn every four days. The invasive presence of the lionfish has had a significant negative impact on indigenous aquatic life, the fishing industry, and even the general health and well-being of an already-strained commercial fishing market.[12]

The hardy but harmful eggs and larvae of a lionfish are also capable of traveling great distances in the ocean currents. This means that lionfish eggs which are fertilized in the waters of the Bahamas are capable of reaching the New England coast of the United States on the Gulf Stream current. Lionfish are indiscriminate and ruthless predators that have consumed up to 70 percent of local fish species and a vast majority of invertebrates in the Bahamas. They can reduce juvenile fish populations by a rate up to about 90 percent. Their stomachs can support volumes that measure up to thirty times their own mass. In some cases, up to 30 mature fish have been found inside the stomachs of one lionfish.

Although dangerous and uniquely destructive, lionfish are quite delicious, so if you want to beat them, why not just eat them? Lionfish contain high quantities of omega three and are extremely low in mercury metals, making them a healthier choice than some of their over-fished and processed alternatives.[13] If you choose to switch your diet to nothing but lionfish, aquatic life in the Bahamas will definitely benefit from your choice. So will the reef and native fish populations, as the more lionfish consumed, the fewer there are in the oceans to terrorize and eat them.

When hunting lionfish, it is wise to have a zookeeper device in which you can store the captured fish. This reduces the chances of you getting any serious injury or infection from their venomous spines. When trying to kill

12.   NOAA, 2014
13.   Harrell, 2017

a lionfish, you will want to aim for the gill area so you don't ruin your tasty fillet. Piercing its gill will kill it by suffocation. Some people remove the venomous spines immediately upon harvest and others wait until topside. Whichever method you choose is acceptable, as long as you stay safe against any injury or toxic exposure.

If you prefer to remove the spines of a lionfish before putting it in the zoo-keeper, it is advisable that you use a pair of sea snips to remove them and then fillet the fish, just like you would do with any other. With the abundance of lionfish, and since the other indigenous types of fish are being placed into harvest-limiting seasons, lionfish hunts can make a dive feel much more purposeful and exciting. Also, most groupers and hogfish (other popular species for eating) live in water depths typically over 30 feet, a distance that is quite difficult for the average free diver to manage. Lionfish harvesting can be a fun experience that also contributes to the overall well-being and health of the coral reefs and fish populations that are indigenous to the Bahamian waters.

If a lionfish stings you while you're diving, it is *very* important not to panic, and to swim back up to the surface safely. Of course you should seek medical care if needed, but here are some common first aid strategies to manage a lionfish sting.[14]

1. Inspect and clean the wound thoroughly. Carefully check for any remaining or broken spine fragments. This is important because residual spines could continue to release venom into your system from the glands located in the grooves. The wound site will be very painful, and you may experience other symptoms similar to an allergic reaction.

2. Apply direct pressure to the sting to control the bleeding.

3. Apply hot water (but not so hot that it burns). The venom in a lionfish spine is a combination of protein, a neurotoxin, and a neurotransmitter; it will break down in the presence of heat. Once the venom breaks down, the pain will start to diminish, along with any

---

14.　Harrell, n.d.

other symptoms. You may take a mild painkiller, if you have any access to any.

4. Keep soaking the wound in water that is as hot as your skin can tolerate and seek medical attention as soon as you can.

5. Seek Medical care if needed.

Eat the Adversaries

If you've caught your lionfish and managed to avoid the sting, here are a couple of quick recipes to satisfy the hearty appetite you worked up diving and exploring.

- -

Trusty Rusty's Lionfish Ceviche

10-12 chopped lionfish fillets
6-8 limes, juiced
1-2 lemons, juiced
½ small red onion, minced
1-2 tomatoes, diced
½ red pepper, diced
½ green pepper, diced
1 jalapeno, minced
½ cucumber, seeded and diced
2-3 green onions, sliced thin
1 clove of garlic, finely minced
¼ teaspoon of ginger, finely minced
Kosher salt to taste
2 tablespoons of cilantro

Combine all the ingredients in a large bowl and mix. Refrigerate for about two hours, stirring occasionally. Serve cold in cups or on a beautiful bed of lettuce.

- -

- -

Blackbeard's Blackened Lionfish

4 lionfish fillets
1/4 teaspoon garlic salt
1/4 teaspoon oregano
1/4 teaspoon paprika
1/4 teaspoon ground black pepper
1/4 teaspoon cayenne pepper
4 tablespoons butter, divided

Preheat your grill or pan. Combine oregano, paprika, black pepper, and cayenne pepper in a small bowl and mix together. Rub the spice mix over the lionfish fillets and wrap in foil with 1 Tbsp butter each. Cook until fish is white and flaky, just under six minutes. Serve over rice.

- -

Bahamian Style Pan Fried Lionfish

Lime juice
Orange juice
Minced garlic
Cilantro
Lionfish fillets
Flour, for dredging
Salt, to taste
Pepper, to taste

Dredge fillets in flour and season with salt and pepper.

Combine first four ingredients in a bowl. Taste the mixture and adjust ratio to your taste. Generously drizzle over the fillets and pan fry in oil until golden brown. Serve over rice or with russet potatoes.

- -

- -

Papa's Poppers

Lionfish fillets, seasoned to your liking and grilled
Bacon, chopped and cooked
Pickled cherry peppers, halved and seeded
Sharp cheddar cheese
Flour, for dredging
Bisquick batter, for dipping

Stuff the peppers with the cheese, bacon, and fish. Dredge the stuffed pepper in flour, then dip into batter and deep-fry until golden brown. Serve with a marinara dipping sauce

- -

COMMON FISH OF BIMINI

Once you make that daring plunge into Bimini's expansive underwater world, you will be met with an explosion of brilliantly vibrant colors from the reef fish that surround you. This portion of the book serves as a guide to the different types of reef fish that you should expect to see. You will learn to identify some of the fish that will be darting around you. The species of fish that populate the reefs of Bimini are seemingly numberless, but here is a list of some to look for as you scout the reefs, coral walls, and wrecks that make up this awe-inspiring area. What could be more fun than keeping track of and learning about your favorite fish while exploring these crystal-clear waters? Enjoy!

Nassau Grouper

Size: Adults can grow to about a maximum size of 4 feet

Depth Range: Can be found in water depths ranging from 20 to 130 feet

About: The Nassau grouper belongs to the sea bass family and is one of the largest fish seen around coral heads. The population is a favorite of local diets and suffered from overfishing in the 20th century. Also in danger from the lionfish epidemic, it is protected by the Ministry of Fisheries - no fishing December through February (always double check local fishing rules). Nassau groupers can be identified by their five brown vertical stripes, which are dual purpose: a form of communication, indicating where they are in the mating cycle by making their stripes brighter or duller, and also a defensive mechanism to blend in with surroundings. When threatened, groupers make a "whop whop" noise to alert other groupers.

Date Seen: _____

Location: _____

Notes: _____

_____

Black Grouper

Size: Adults can grow to a maximum size of 4 feet
Depth Range: Can be found in water depths ranging from 20 to 130 feet

About: The black grouper is a solitary fish with grey blotches on its body. The outer third of the second dorsal and anal fins are completely black. Like the Nassau grouper, the population has suffered due to over-fishing and due to the presence of the invasive lionfish. All black groupers are born female, and some transform into males when they are large enough.

Date Seen: _____

Location: _____

Notes: _____

_____

Tiger Grouper

Size: Adults grow to a maximum of 2 feet
Depth Range: Can be found in depths ranging from 20 to 60 feet

About: Tiger groupers are reddish in color and are highly unique because they are the only grouper species with 9-11 pale stripes that angle down and taper, like the stripes on a tiger. They are known for their habit of launching surprise attacks on their prey. They usually hide in holes in the reef, waiting patiently for small juvenile fish to swim by. When they sight potential prey, they use powerful suction to draw them into their mouths. They are one of the prettiest groupers to look at, with stunning streamlined bodies.

Date Seen: _____
Location: _____
Notes: _____
_____

Queen Parrot

Size: Adults grow to a maximum size of 1foot
Depth Range: Can be found in depths from 20 to 60 feet

About: Queen parrot fish have two color phases: dull as youngsters, they are gray with a broad white stripe along their sides; and bright when mature, they are iridescent green, blue, purple, orange, and yellow. Parrot fish get their name from their beak-like mouths, which scrape algae and plants from the reef's surface. The Queen, like most other parrot fish, secretes a mucus cocoon to sleep in at night. If you are lucky enough to see this phase on a night dive, please do not disturb it. It is a time-consuming and difficult process for the parrot fish to complete, and while it is out of the cocoon it may be highly vulnerable to a wide array of predators.

Date Seen: _____
Location: _____
Notes: _____
_____

Midnight Parrot

Size: Adults grow to a maximum size of 3 feet
Depth Range: Can be found in depths up to 80 feet

About: The Midnight Parrotfish is deep blue in color and likes to swim over sandy areas. They use their large teeth to scrape algae off of coral to feed on. Younger, smaller, not as colorful males will fertilize the eggs of one female with several other males. Larger males with their own territory will fertilize the eggs of one female.

Date Seen: _____
Location: _____
Notes: _____
_____

Stoplight Parrot

Size: Adults grow to a maximum size of 1-2 feet
Depth Range: Can be found in depths from 15 to 80 feet

About: These parrot fish are identified by their greed, red, and yellow accents. They like to inhabit low-lying reef while feeding on algae and coral.

Date Seen: _____
Location: _____
Notes: _____
_____

Four Eye Butterfly Fish

Size: Adults grow to a maximum size of 6 inches
Depth Range: Can be found in depths ranging from10 to 60 feet

About: The four eye butterfly fish are very common among the reefs of the Bahamas and are often seen moving in pairs because they choose their mates for life. If you see a group of three, just swim quietly away and save yourself the awkwardness. As a small fish, they need to employ some tricks to stay safe, so they have a false eye on their tail which is there to confuse would-be predators.

Date Seen: _____

Location: _____

Notes: _____

_____

Scorpion Fish

Size: Adults grow to a maximum of 1 foot
Depth Range: Can be found in depths ranging from 10 to 60 feet

About: These guys are the masters of camouflage. They are bottom dwellers that are very difficult to spot, due to their rock-like appearance and coloration. They are patient predators, and are so well disguised that small juvenile fish swim by close enough to end up getting sucked into their powerful mouths. As a defense mechanism, they have spines along their dorsal fins that inject a neurotoxin into their predators, causing excruciating pain. You should definitely be careful around these. Don't get stung!

Date Seen: _____

Location: _____

Notes: _____

_____

Hogfish

Size: Adults grow to be a maximum of 3 feet
Depth Range: Can be found in depths ranging from 10 to 130 feet

About: The hogfish can be identified by their unique pig-like snouts and three long tines on the forward part of their dorsal area. They use their snouts to search through the sand for buried crustaceans. They are also sequential hermaphrodites, and an alpha male will have harems of up to 10 females flocking around him. If that alpha male should get speared (a common occurrence since hogfish are highly delicious), the beta female will actually change sex to become the new alpha male of the harem. What a crazy life cycle!

Date Seen: _____

Location: _____

Notes: _____

_____

French Angelfish

Size: Adults grow to be a maximum of 3 feet
Depth Range: Can be found in depths ranging from 10 to 130 feet

About: The French Angelfish does not have an accent or wear a beret. They mate for life so they are commonly seen moving in pairs. If one should lose a mate, it will not take on another. They can be found in shallow reefs feeding on sponges and algae. They are highly territorial and a French Angelfish will defend its territory at all costs.

Date Seen: _____

Location: _____

Notes: _____

_____

Queen Angelfish

Size: Adults grow to be a maximum of 17 inches
Depth Range: Can be found in depths ranging from 10 to 70 feet

About: The Queen Angelfish gets its name from the royal blue color and blue spot on its forehead, which resembles a crown. They have dazzling blue bodies with fiery yellow and purple accents. They are a shy fish but are incredibly beautiful to look at and will definitely provide you with some awesome memories and photographs. Juveniles will set themselves up on cleaning stations, often cleaning parasites off of larger fish.

Date Seen: _____

Location: _____

Notes: _____

_____

Southern Stingray

Size: Adults grow to be a maximum of 3 feet
Depth Range: Can be found at depths ranging from 3 to 130 feet

About: The Southern Stingray has a flat, spade-shaped body, with a long tail that has a barb covered in venomous mucus. As you admire these amazing animals, remember that one of these killed the Crocodile Hunter, Steve Irwin. It is highly recommended that you keep your distance and give them their space. They have adapted to life on the ocean floor, and spend their time feeding on small fish, worms, and crustaceans.

Date Seen: _____

Location: _____

Notes: _____

_____

Yellow Stingray

Size: Adults grow to be a maximum of 14 inches
Depth Range: Can be found in depths ranging from 3 to 80 feet

About: The Yellow Stingray is more disc-shaped than the southern stingray. Yellow stingrays have a yellow and black speckled pattern. This helps them to effectively ambush their prey. Also, they have a small venomous spine near their tail which acts as a defense mechanism against potential predators.

Date Seen: _____

Location: _____

Notes: _____

_____

Spotted Moray Eel

Size: Adults can grow to be a maximum of 6 feet
Depth Range: Can be found in depths ranging from 10 to 130 feet

About: These are solitary animals that wind themselves through the cracks and holes of corals with their heads peeking out. They have poor eyesight and feed only on small fish and crusta-ceans. Their teeth are angled backwards to prevent prey from escaping their bite.

Date Seen: _____

Location: _____

Notes: _____

_____

Yellow Head Jawfish

Size: Adults can grow to a maximum of 4 inches
Depth Range: Can be found in depts ranging from 3 to 130 feet

About: Yellow Head Jawfish are an industrious fish, using their mouths as scoops to dig and move small rocks to make holes for hiding in the sand. They usually don't stray far from their hole and when threatened, they immediately retreat into the hole for protection. The male jawfish will store eggs in its mouth until they have hatched.

Date Seen: _____

Location: _____

Notes: _____

_____

Blue Chromis

Size: Adults can grow to a maximum of 5 inches
Depth Range: Can be found in depths up to a maximum of 60 feet

About: These beauties can be seen in huge schools throughout the dive sites of Bimini. They feed on zooplankton and belong to the damsel fish family.

Date Seen: _____

Location: _____

Notes: _____

_____

Scrawled File Fish

Size: Adults can grow to be a maximum of 3 feet
Depth Range: Can be found in depths of up to 130 feet

About: The Scrawled File Fish can be seen on a lot of reefs in Bimini and is usually easy to spot due to its odd-shaped, compressed body. Its colors are a greenish-yellow with blue dots and lines. Their skin is so rough that years ago, sailors would use it to strike matches on. They tend to shy away from divers and blend into the surrounding rocks.[15]

Date Seen: _____

Location: _____

Notes: _____

_____

Flamingo Tongue

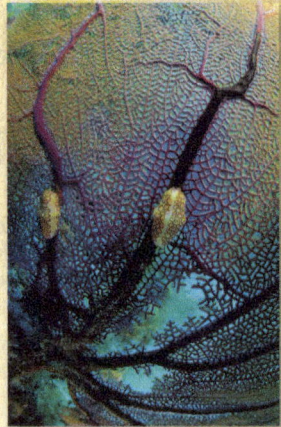

Size: Adults can grow to be a maximum of 4 inches
Depth Range: Can be found in depths ranging from 3 to 130 feet

About: These mollusks live and feed on sea fans and soft corals. They are quite difficult to spot at first, but once you find one, you will probably find several more close by. Their orange spots make for great photographs.

Date Seen: _____

Location: _____

Notes: _____

_____

15.   Answers in Genesis, n.d.

CREATURES OF THE NIGHT

A lot of new divers are put off by the notion of diving under water at night. So why would you want to bother diving at night? While we watch the sun go down from the surface, the environment beneath is changing completely. A whole new multitude of fish are "changing shift". Many of the fish, especially the smaller tropicals, are settling into nooks and crannies to rest and hide from predators. Coral polyps open up to catch zoo plankton nearby while the appendages of basket stars begin to unfold to feel the current and search for food. You may even catch an octopus crawling across the reef.

One of my favorite things on a night dive is the bioluminescence. By covering your light and waving your hand around you will see a pixie dust or firefly effect, which is actually agitated bacteria emitting this light through a chemical change in their body.

On a night dive you have a light and a back up so you are constantly reintroducing artificial light to the area. During the day the color red is typically reduced after 15 or 20 feet so now with your dive light you are introducing many of the colors into the area that are typically lost during a day dive.

A night dive is a truly unique and amazing way to experience the underwater world. Keep a look out for some of these amazing creatures. Remember a lot of these animals are sleeping or resting, so try to avoid shining your light directly in their faces.

Octopus

Size: 1 inches to a maximum of 3 feet
Depth Range: 15 to 75 feet

About: Octopuses are pretty recognizable with their large head, often called a mantle, eyes and eight arms with suckers on the underside. They are highly intelligent sea creatures and masters of camouflage -- they can change the color of their skin in less than half a second -- and mimic its surroundings. It literally looks as if it appears and disappears. Scientist have observed these creatures opening child proof pill bottles.

Date Seen: _____

Location: _____

Notes: _____

_____

Spanish Lobster

Size: 6 to 12 inches
Depth Range: 30 to 130 feet

About: These guys are typically reddish to orang-ish brown in color. Their bodies on the forward section usually have four or five purple spots with yellow legs. They hide in holes during the day and brave the night to forage and look for food. If they feel threatened they can swim backward very quickly with strokes from their power-ful tails.

Date Seen: _____

Location: _____

Notes: _____

_____

Parrot Fish

Size: Adults grow to a maximum size of 1foot
Depth Range: 20 to 60 feet

About: When a parrot fish decides it is time to go to bed, it makes a sleeping bag by secreting its own mucus from glands in its gills. This forms a protective barrier enveloping its entire body. This process accomplishes two things: it hides their scent from predators and acts like a trip wire alarm. If a predator touches its cocoon, the parrot fish is alerted and can swim off to safety. If you witness this amazing process do not disturb it because it is a lot of work for the parrot fish to create that membrane sleeping bag.

Date Seen: _____

Location: _____

Notes: _____

_____

Caribbean Reef Squid

Size: 6-12 inches
Depth Range: Up to 60 feet

About: These squid can be identified by their oblong body that has a thin fin which tapers to a point at their rear. Their color ranges from a translucent blue during the day to brown with mottled white spots at night. They are generally apprehensive of divers and will back away slowly, but will dart away if they feel threatened. You can often spot these guys before you jump in on night dives because they are usually attracted to the lights of the boat.

Date Seen: _____

Location: _____

Notes: _____

_____

Brittle Star

Size: Up to a maximum size of 4 inches
Depth Range: 3 to 130 feet

About: Members of the starfish family, they have five long, whip-like arms extending from their center. When a Brittle Star moves, one of its arms points the way forward, and arms on the left and right start a rowing-like movement. When it turns, it doesn't turn its entire body, it just chooses a new lead arm. They are very quick and tend to dart way from lights on night dives. Keep that in mind if you spot one.

Date Seen: _____

Location: _____

Notes: _____

_____

Giant Basket Star

Size: 1 inch
Depth Range: 1 to 130 feet

About: Basket Stars have five arms stretching out from their center and sub-branches coming off each incredibly flexible arm over and over again to form a kind of mesh-like basket. During the day these arms and branches are balled up and they sometimes hide inside sponges or just lay on the ground. They need an adequate current. Typically at night they will unfurl that mesh ball and with an arm grab on to a piece of coral and grab small plankton with the other arm to put into their mouth. Then branches look really nasty close up through a macro lens, but they are amazing creatures to look out for on a night dive.

Date Seen: _____

Location: _____

Notes: _____

_____

Banded Coral Shrimp

Size: 1 to 2 inches
Depth Range: 3 to 130 feet

About: These shrimp can be spotted near the openings of coral and sponges. They have a red and white banded body with hair-like antennas. They also have a pair of claws for defense and hunting.

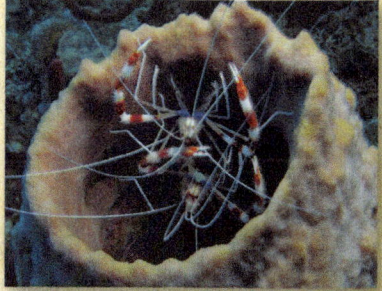

Date Seen: _____

Location: _____

Notes: _____

_____

SEA TURTLES

Scientists believe sea turtles have been around for well over 100 million years. Their shells have developed their streamlined shape to make swimming through the water easier. Unlike their land-dwelling cousins, they cannot retract their legs and heads into their shells for protection. They feed primarily on jellyfish, shrimp, and sponges. Depending on how active the turtle may be or if it is threatened, they can comfortably stay under water up to four or five hours.

Most species of sea turtles reach sexual maturity from ages two to five years old. Female sea turtles will return to the same beach where they were hatched to lay their own eggs there.

Depending on her species, she can deposit between 50 to 200 eggs at one time. With her back flippers, she digs a hole in the sand and buries her entire clutch of eggs. The gestation period for the eggs is between 6-10 weeks. The mother never returns to check on her eggs or young, but when they emerge from the sand, always at night, they instinctively head for the ocean. Sadly, only about 10 percent of the eggs will survive the dangerous journey to adulthood. Many of them end up as lunch for birds or other wildlife. And let's not forget the human element, which likes to develop oceanfront properties and/or collect turtle eggs for food.

There are three types of sea turtles you may see during your diving adventures in Bimini:

Hawksbill

The Hawksbill turtle can grow to be up to three and a half feet long. They get their name from their defined beak which bears a striking resemblance to that of a hawk. Their shells were very desirable at one time, and turtles were killed so humans could use their shells to decorate furniture, jewelry, souvenirs, fans, and combs. Due to this and some natural factors, their numbers have rapidly declined over the years and most countries have put a trade ban on any products made from turtles in order to save them from extinction.

Date Seen: _____

Location: _____

Notes: _____

_____

Green

Green turtles are born only two inches long and can reach sizes of up to five feet as they mature. They are named for the greenish hue of their skin. With their streamlined shell and strong fins, they have been known to achieve speeds of up to 35 miles an hour in the water! They look so effortless and graceful and are quite a sight to behold, especially when moving in groups.

Date Seen: _____

Location: _____

Notes: _____

_____

Loggerhead

These turtles are endowed with the toughest shells of all sea turtle shells. They are quite massive, and can reach sizes of over three feet and weigh of up to 250 pounds. They are called "loggerhead" because of the large size and shape of their heads. Loggerheads have mighty jaws which are capable of eating conch shells! Their typical dive time is between 15-30 minutes, and a maximum of up to four hours depending on how active they are at that moment. They feed on soft corals, jellyfish, and crustaceans.

Date Seen: _____

Location: _____

Notes: _____

_____

DOLPHINS

The ocean's most social mammal can often be seen riding on the bow wakes of boats in the Bimini area. They are amazingly fast and incredibly playful swimmers that love to jump and somersault through the air. Atlantic spotted and bottlenose dolphins are the two common species in the Bimini area (though pan-tropical spotteds are often seen in the Gulf Stream). Of the two species, the spotted dolphins have been discovered to be more interested in humans. The Atlantic spotted dolphins are thought to be lifelong residents of the Bimini area; researchers are still learning about the bottlenose dolphins' comings and goings. The older spotted dolphins have spots which are distinct and almost Dalmatian-like. The number of spots increases as the dolphin ages. Spotted dolphin calves are born with slightly two-toned grey skin and they measure between 35 to 40 inches in length. Around the time they are weaned from their mothers, speckling begins to occur. As the dolphin matures, the spotting begins to appear more dense until it covers their entire bodies. At full maturity, spotted dolphins are over 7 feet long and may weigh upwards of 300 pounds. Compared with other species of dolphins, they would be medium sized. The largest dolphins are actually orcas, which can reach over 30 feet in size!

Bottlenose dolphins are a little more recognizable due to the fact that they can be seen in marine parks, documentaries, and television programs. They are grey with blueish grey shading. These dolphins share habitats at times with the spotted dolphin. Contrary to popular belief, they usually are not quite as interactive as their spotted friends. A bottlenose calf is typically about 40-50 inches long, while a bottlenose adult can reach up to 8 or 9 feet in length and weigh anywhere from 300 to 1,000 pounds. The bottlenose dolphins seen in the Bimini area are considered small in comparison to those seen in other locations.

Just like us humans, dolphins need to breathe air. The difference between our respiratory system and theirs is that they do it through a nostril or a blowhole that is located on the top of their head. This allows them to just expose the tops of their heads on the water's surface for respiration while they are swimming or resting. After each breath, the hole is sealed tightly to keep water from getting into their lungs. This allows them to eat while underwater, as their respiratory system is not connected to their esophagus, like it is for humans.

Some dolphins will cooperate when hunting and feeding. First, they'll encircle a large school of fish, then each dolphin takes a turn swimming through the entrapped school to feed. Sometimes they push the schools into shallow water where they become very easy prey. Dolphins do not chew their food before swallowing; small fish they swallow whole, and they shake or rub large prey on the ocean floor until the pieces become manageable and can fit into their beaks. Dolphins have several stomachs to break down their food. Adult bottlenose dolphins can consume four to six percent of their body weight in a day. Adult spotted dolphins can consume two to four percent of their weight.

Bottlenose and spotted dolphins can be seen in many areas of Bimini, and the Dolphin Communication Project (DCP) has been researching and studying these animals for over 16 years. The DCP was founded by Kathleen Dudzinski who, from 1991 to 2002, was researching spotted dolphins off the island of Grand Bahama. She spent six months a year on a boat observing these magnificent mammals and even participated in the making of the famous IMAX film *Dolphins*. While she was working on the film, she observed the resident community of spotted dolphins off Bimini and began to collaborate with Bimini Undersea (a local scuba diving outfit) and helped launch a systematic study of the dolphins. It was after the release of the film in 2000 that she founded the DCP.

In 2003, Kelly Melillo Sweeting and Kat DeStefano were interns for the DCP. Kelly eventually became the site manager of the field site in Bimini, and since then has been very passionate about promoting the study of dolphins to better understand them and to inspire their conservation. She has created opportunities for the public to engage in dolphin science through eco-tours, volunteering, and internships. They even have an amazing "Adopt-a-Dolphin" program. By using special video and audio equipment, they have been able to identify and catalog Bimini's community of dolphins. By adopting one of these dolphins, you provide funds for the DCP to use for education, research, and conservation efforts. There are hardcopy and electronic adoption kits available that come with an Adoption Certificate, a photograph of your dolphin, its biography, and a video of the Bimini dolphins. To learn more, go to www.dolphincommunicationproject.org

The Dolphin Code of Conduct

While visiting Bimini, especially during the summer months, it is highly recommended that you choose an outfitter or a tour guide to help you see the dolphins, and it's important that they follow the Dolphin Code of Conduct. If you come upon the dolphins on your own, please respect them and all wildlife in the area, and follow and share this code.

1) Operate your vessel at a speed of 8 knots or less when in you are in close proximity to dolphin groups.

2) Observe dolphin groups from the surface to determine their general behavior. Do not, under any circumstance, allow swimmers to enter the water if the group appears to be resting. Resting is typically shown by slow group movement at or near the surface, with limited interactions between the dolphins in the group, no direction or speed changes, no aerial behaviors, no bow riding, and slow or splashless breaths. If the dolphins are bottom feeding, the human swimmers are allowed to only watch from the surface. If the dolphins are feeding at the surface or in mid-water (i.e., feeding in a way that is different from bottom feeding), swimmers are prohibited from entering the water. If the dolphins are actively mating, human swimmers should observe from a distance without directly interacting with the dolphins in any way.

3) The number of vessels interacting with a single dolphin group is limited to one for the safety of both the dolphins and human swimmers involved, unless adequate radio communication has been established. If radio contact is not established, a vessel should stay at least half a mile away from another vessel while interacting with the dolphins.

4) Do not circle if the dolphin group appears to be feeding or resting, and under no circumstance should you make repetitive tight circles.

5) Before any voyage or expedition, every operator should ensure that they give an educational talk to all human swimmers. This talk should include this code of conduct before their first dolphin swim. The most important pieces of information that should be passed are:

   a) DO NOT touch the dolphins at any time whatsoever. If at any point a dolphin initiates contact with a human swimmer, this should not be taken as an invitation to touch the dolphin back. Swimmers are encouraged to swim with their hands at their sides, across their chests or behind their backs, so as to eliminate the risk of making physical contact with the dolphins.

   b) You should try as much as possible to limit horizontal swimming so as not to actively pursue the dolphins. Vertical swimming is acceptable, provided that the swimmers are conscious of the presence of other swimmers and dolphins as they return to the surface.

6) In order to monitor the interactions with the dolphins and to protect them, there should be one trained crew member in the water per 12 swimmers, and a maximum of 25 persons in the water at the same time.

7) All human swimmers should enter the water in a calm and quiet manner while being in close proximity to the dolphins. No large splashes or sudden jumping into the water.

8) No foreign objects aside from floatation devices and camera equipment will be brought into the water with the dolphins.

9) If the dolphins turn away or change direction a third time during an attempt to approach, then the vessel should immediately move on.

10) No flash photography after the sun has set, so as not to startle the dolphins.

11) No sounds or music will be played under water.

12) Adhere to the strict "no feeding" policy!

13) All waste must be returned to shore with the vessel.

14) An overall effort must be made in order to discourage private boaters and non-established operators from seeking interactions with the dolphins. No one agreeing to these guidelines shall give such boaters assistance or advice, nor serve as a guide, in finding dolphins.

15) All interested tourists are encouraged to sign up with an experienced local operator who is authorized to take walk-in guests and is in agreement with this code of conduct.

16) Any stranded or entangled dolphins (or other marine mammals, including sea turtles) will be reported to the Bahamas Marine Mammal Stranding Network: (242) 347-3033 or (242) 366-4155.

17) These guidelines will be reviewed annually and changes will be made in response to changes in policies, administration, and any other structural adjustments.

Spotted Dolphin

Date Seen: _____
Location: _____
Notes: _____
_____
_____
_____
_____
_____
_____
_____
_____
_____
_____

Bottlenose Dolphin

Date Seen: _____
Location: _____
Notes: _____
_____
_____
_____
_____
_____
_____
_____
_____
_____

SHARKS!

The Bahamas is considered to be the shark capital of the world. Diving is a huge part of their tourism industry and Bimini is naturally a large part of it. Just the word "shark" is enough to send a shiver up one's spine, but many scientists and enthusiasts believe these creatures are largely and grossly misunderstood. Only about five people die each year from shark attacks worldwide, while millions die from starvation. Let's put that into perspective. You have more of a chance of being killed by a coconut falling out of a tree and crashing directly on to your head while you're distracted taking a selfie than being attacked by a shark. Most shark incidents are cases of mistaken identity.

Bimini has arranged organized shark feeds since the late 1970s, and the Bimini area has been an integral part of the longest running study of sharks to date. Dr. Samuel Gruber began studying lemon sharks in the mangroves of Bimini's North Sound in the late 1980s. He founded the Bimini Biological Field Station (BBFS), also known as the Shark Lab, in 1990. The research efforts organized by these people have since evolved from just lemon sharks to include all species of shark that are indigenous to the area. Shark Lab also discovered one of only two known great hammerhead aggregations in the world in Bimini. Shark Lab is an amazing organization which puts together extensive outreach and educational programs. They give tours with a suggested donation of $10 per person, which supports their research endeavors. If you're interested in contacting them, they are always on standby on VHF channel 88a, or you can contact them by phone at (242) 347-4538. If you're a dive enthusiast and shark lover, then a visit to Shark Lab is a must do -- it is a interactive, hands-on tour. It's highly entertaining and very educational.

When it comes to sharks and diving, the word "infested" gets thrown about too often. Even diving up to four times a day, you may only see a shark once per week, and that would normally only happen near one of the organized feed sites. You definitely want to take precautions spearfishing and always keep your two eyes open; always use the buddy system when swimming or doing anything in the open ocean. There is no reason to be overcome with fear upon seeing a shark. It should be respected and taken in as a beautiful moment that only a select few ever get to experience.

Organized shark feeds

If you're looking to kick your scuba diving thrill meter up a notch, then there is no better way than an organized shark feed. It may be just what you are looking for. Once you're in the water among the sharks, you will probably feel a mix of terror and enchantment. One thing is for sure: If you do decide to embark on this adventure, it will most surely be a memory of a lifetime and will earn its place on your Bahamas Bucket List. There is a strict protocol put in place for organized feeds that varies from species to species, and from outfitter to outfitter. If you strictly adhere to the briefing, you will have absolutely nothing to worry about.

Neal Watson's Bimini Scuba Center is a top-notch outfitter and will certainly make sure that your bucket list dive goes off without a hitch. It doesn't matter if you're a diving novice; he and his staff of highly-skilled professionals will make certain that you and all your needs are taken care of from the moment you board the *Dive God,* Neal's well-laid-out day dive boat.

Ideally, you will depart from the fuel dock at the Big Game Club on North Bimini around 11 a.m. You'll make the short trip to the *Hammer Headquarters* and once you get there, they will search for the right spot to anchor the boat for the feed. At this point, it's time to prepare for the dive. The set-up can take anywhere from five minutes to a few hours. Once the hammerheads are drawn in with chum and the sharks and staff are comfortable, you will be invited into the water. The hard bottom floor of this watery area is around twenty feet, so you can really focus on these majestic creatures as they pass by within an arms reach. That said, you'll definitely want to have a camera to collect a few souvenirs of this amazing and awe-inspiring moment. Once you've hit your tank limit, you should return to the vessel where it is recommended that you get some rest, hydrate, and fix yourself something nice to eat before getting back into the water. The dive day will last until they run out of chum, bait, tanks, or daylight. Once this awesome experience is over, you'll be returned to the shore, but the memories of this experience will remain with you always.

It is important to note that this feed is seasonal and goes from December through April. The water temperature in Bimini ranges from the low to mid 70s. This piece of information should help you plan your dive trip accordingly. A wetsuit with a density of at least 5 mm is recommended due to the long nature of the dive. Hoods and gloves are also required for protection. Onshore there is top quality and state-of-the-art dive gear available to rent, however, tanks and weights are provided free-of-charge, if you go through the proper channels. For more information about planning, site availability, and any other materials that you may need, please feel free to visit www.biminiscubacenter.com.

Here are some of the sharks you may encounter as you endeavor to complete your Bimini Dive Bucket List:

Nurse Shark

The Nurse Shark is one of the more common shark species you will encounter. They are the only shark that can lie still while at the same time still not forcing the influx of water through their gills to breathe.[16] Their size can range between four to fifteen feet. They are bottom-dwellers that suck crustaceans, mollusks, and small fish into their mouths. Females usually have up to thirty pups, which may sound like a lot, but often the stronger pups eat the under-developed ones, so the entire litter doesn't make it to adulthood. It is a sobering demonstration of survival of the fittest.

Date Seen: _____

Location: _____

Notes: _____

_____

Reef Shark

Reef Sharks are pretty common in Bimini and can be found on almost any dive. They are passive in most contexts but can get curious if a spearfishing expedition is getting too close. If you're spearfishing and see their pectoral fins drop and they begin quick, darting movements, it is best just to give the shark the fish and move on. These sharks have keen eyesight to see in murky waters, specialized organs in their head to detect electric vibrations, and an excellent sense of smell to prey on bony fish. They can get as big as eight feet, and weigh around 150 pounds.

Date Seen: _____

Location: _____

Notes: _____

_____

---

16.   Castro, 2013

Bull Shark

Classified as #3 on the list of most dangerous sharks in the world, the bull shark is a pretty rare sight to see. They can reach up to 13 feet in length and weigh over 1,000 pounds on average. One unique thing about bull sharks is they can live and thrive in both fresh and salt water due to a process called osmoregulation. These sharks aren't picky eaters -- they will eat a variety of fish, rays, turtles, and even other sharks. The females are the larger of the species and can have between four and six pups, which are immediately left to survive on their own after birth.

Date Seen: _____

Location: _____

Notes: _____

_____

Tiger Shark

The Tiger Shark has the second most recorded number of attacks on humans in history (only surpassed by the Great White) and it is the fourth largest shark in the world. They are very curious and will eat just about anything -- clothing, tires, books, and even license plates have been found in their stomachs. So if you encounter one, give it a wide berth. Tiger sharks can grow to 20 feet long and weigh anywhere from 800 to 1500 pounds. As a general rule, never turn your back on a tiger shark, and always use the buddy system.

Date Seen: _____

Location: _____

Notes: _____

_____

Great Hammerhead

The Great Hammerhead is one of the most elusive sharks, but its T-shaped head is unmistakable. It gives them a wide field of vision, and a distinct advantage when biting their prey -- they keep an eye on their prey while feasting. Bimini is home to one of two known aggregations in the world. Your odds of seeing them are best between late December and late April, when they come to Bimini for mating. Their diet consists mainly of stingrays, and sometimes, they might have several stingray spines lodged in their mouths without being hindered. They are also known to eat fish, crabs, lobsters, octopuses, and occasionally other smaller sharks.

Date Seen: _____

Location: _____

Notes: _____

_____

Lemon Shark

The name "Lemon Shark" is truly an odd name for a shark, but it comes from the yellow hue in their skin. Bimini is the site of one of the longest-running studies on the lemon shark. Lemon sharks can be found in groups. There have been only 29 known attacks on humans by Lemon sharks worldwide, with each and every victim surviving. Lemon sharks depend on their sense of smell and an electromagnetic sense to seek out their prey. They swim great distances to mate, and females like to pup in the shallow water of the mangrove areas of Bimini, giving their litter of four to fourteen pups maximum protection for their first crucial years of life.

Date Seen: _____

Location: _____

Notes: _____

_____

DIVE LOG BOOK

NORTH BIMINI TO NORTH CAT CAY

The dive sites in this area are beautiful and well within reach of most day boat operations on the island. You see north and south Bimini as you cruise along the Gulf Stream's edge to your dive site for the day. The sites in this region range from wrecks to reefs, and include the infamous "Lost Road to Atlantis."

Skill Level Key	
BEGINNER	⊕
NOVICE	⊕ ⊕
ADVANCED	⊕ ⊕ ⊕

Dive Outfitter Key

Will indicate that the site can be reached with a day boat
By these outfitters.

Operator: Bimini Big Game Club PADI Dive Center
Email: dive@biggameclubbimini.com
Website: http://www.biggameclubbimini.com
Reservations: 800-867-4764

Operator: Bimini Undersea
Email: ebriones68@gmail.com
Website: www.biminiundersea.com
Reservations: 786-462-4641

Operator: Neal Watsons Bimini Scuba Center
Email: dive@biminisands.com
Website: www.biminisands.com
Reservations: 800-737-1007

This will indicate the site can be accessed by a liveaboard
dive operation.

Juliet Sailing and Diving
123 SE 3rd Ave #484
Miami, FL 33131
866-558-5438

1) Half Pipe or Nekton Wall

Max Depth: 130 feet

Location: 1.5 miles east of North Rock

Synopsis: A coral wall starting out in 60' water and steeply dropping to 120'-130'. The site is prone to current and the best time to dive it is about 2 hours after a slack high tide. The reef runs north to south for around 900 feet. It doesn't make a great drift. You definitely want to try another dive site if there is current, which can rip. African Pomano and the occasional hammerhead have been spotted cruising through this dive.

Date: _____   *Dive #:* _____

Max Depth: _____   *Dive Outfitters:* 🛢️ ⛵

Camera: _____

Skill Level: ☸ ☸ ☸   *Lionfish speared:* _____

Notes: _____

_____

_____

_____

_____

_____

_____

_____

_____

┌─────────────────┐
│   │
│   │
│   Boat Stamp   │
│   │
│   │

Signature: _____

Buddy Signature: _____

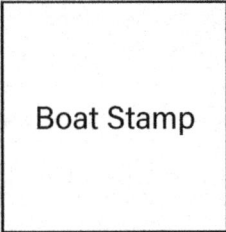

2) The Wreck of the Hesperus

Max Depth: 20 feet

Location: Approximately 13 miles east of North Rock

Synopsis: This is a scattered, impenetrable wreck that sits in about 20' of water. The fish traffic here is amazing, with schools of yellowtail snappers and grunts, but the real attraction is the turtles. The history of the wreck is unknown but is named after the famed Rudyard Kipling poem. Huge loggerhead turtles love to call this site home, so make sure you have your camera ready!

Date: _____   Dive #: _____

Max Depth: _____   Dive Outfitters:

Camera: _____

Skill Level: Lionfish speared: _____

Notes: _____

_____

_____

_____

_____

_____

_____

_____

_____

Signature: _____

Buddy Signature: _____

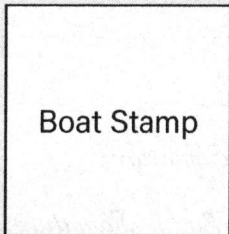

Boat Stamp

3) *Hawksbill Reef*

Max Depth: 85 feet

Location: West of Three Sisters Rocks

Synopsis: Scattered medium- to high-profile coral heads teeming with fish life. It is rare to see hawksbill turtles here, but not unheard of. You can still see plenty of Bermuda chubs, jacks, and the occasional nurse shark. These eye-catching coral heads will keep you mesmerized throughout your dive.

Date: _____   *Dive #:* _____

Max Depth: _____   *Dive Outfitters:* 🛢️ ⛵

Camera: _____

Skill Level: ☸   *Lionfish speared:* _____

Notes: _____

_____

_____

_____

_____

_____

_____

_____

_____   ┌─────────────┐
                                                  │   │
Signature: _____   │ Boat Stamp │
                                                  │   │
Buddy Signature: _____   └─────────────┘

4) Moray Alley

Max Depth: 45 feet

Location: 1 mile west of Three Sisters Rocks

Synopsis: Scattered medium-profile coral heads. This reef has morays, angelfish of all varieties, and schools of yellowtail snapper. It is a large site, so don't stray far from the boat unless you're experienced at navigation.

Date: _____   *Dive #:* _____

Max Depth: _____   *Dive Outfitters:* 🛢️ ⛵

Camera: _____

Skill Level: ☸️ ☸️   *Lionfish speared:* _____

Notes: _____

_____

_____

_____

_____

_____

_____

_____

_____

Signature: _____

Buddy Signature: _____

Boat Stamp

5) Lost Road to Atlantis

Max Depth: 20 feet

Location: 1/4 mile north of Three Sisters Rocks

Synopsis: This site has been featured on shows including *In Search Of* and the History Channel's *Ancient Aliens*. I've met some very rational people who claim The Bimini Road is part of the lost city of Atlantis. Some say the enormous flat stones are ballast stones from ancient boats. Some are sure it's a portal to another universe.

Whatever you believe, it is a decent dive, especially for beginners, and a spectacular snorkel. These are 6 foot by 3 foot rectangular blocks running in a line from north to south. You can decide for yourself if ancient aliens made them or if it's a freeway leading to Atlantis. This is one of the few places in the Bimini area where you may see a flamingo tongue. Other inhabitants include schools of grunts and stingrays.

Date: _____   Dive #: _____

Max Depth: _____   Dive Outfitters:

Camera: _____

Skill Level: ⚙   Lionfish speared: _____

Notes: _____

_____

_____

_____

_____

Signature: _____

Buddy Signature: _____

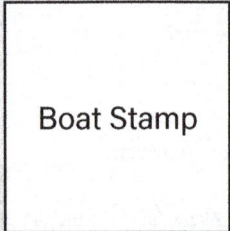

Boat Stamp

6) *The Strip*

Max Depth: 40 feet

Location: West of Radio Beach

Synopsis: A medium-profile reef roughly 200 feet long and 10 feet wide, running north to south. A super-easy site for novice divers to navigate, and inch for inch it's packed with life. A favorite haunt for scorpion fish and an amazing night dive. On a night dive, definitely look for octopuses.

Date: _____   *Dive #:* _____

Max Depth: _____   *Dive Outfitters:*

Camera: _____

Skill Level: *Lionfish speared:* _____

Notes: _____

_____

_____

_____

_____

_____

_____

_____

_____

Signature: _____

Buddy Signature: _____

Boat Stamp

7) *Lewda*

Max Depth: 60 feet

Location: West of Radio Beach

Synopsis: Named after Captain Lew Raymond, aka Lewda. He was famous for his "Lewd-isms", one of which was "No Free Thinking." Lew ran his boat his way and wasn't big on change. He was a great captain and friend. The dive site is scattered medium-profile coral heads and was one of his favorites. Schools of grunts and French angelfish will host your dive and you can certainly keep your eyes open for spotted morays.

Date: _____   *Dive #:* _____

Max Depth: _____   *Dive Outfitters:* 🛢️ ⛵

Camera: _____

Skill Level: ☸   *Lionfish speared:* _____

Notes: _____

_____

_____

_____

_____

_____

_____

_____

_____

_____

Boat Stamp

Signature: _____

Buddy Signature: _____

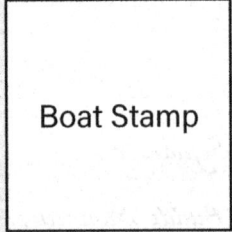

8) *The Barge*

Max Depth: 100 feet

Location: 2 miles due west of old Bimini range markers

Synopsis: The wreck is prone to strong currents because it sits so close to the continental shelf, but it's so worth it. The safest time for diving it is two hours after low tide. The 100-foot barge reportedly sank in the 1980s and is ensconced in coral growth. It is penetrable in various spots, allowing for some amazing photographs. Walls of grunts will part as you make your way through and around the wreck. Keep your eyes out for schools of visiting pompanos and other Pelagics. Sharks have been spotted a few times recently, so hopefully you'll get lucky. The Bimini Barge sits on a sandy bottom with no other items of interest near it. When diving at this site, it's best to stay close due to the current.

Date: _____   *Dive #:* _____

Max Depth: _____   *Dive Outfitters:*

Camera: _____

Skill Level: ⚙ ⚙ ⚙   *Lionfish speared:* _____

Notes: _____

_____

_____

_____

_____

_____

_____

Signature: _____

Buddy Signature: _____

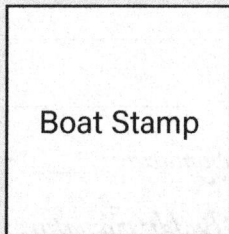

Boat Stamp

9) North Turtle Rocks

Max Depth: 35 feet

Location: If you divide Turtle Rocks into thirds North Turtle would be the portion of the rocks closest to S. Bimini

Synopsis: Don't get too stoked about seeing a turtle here, though it's not unheard of. The rocks are actually named for the brain corals that peek out of the water at low tide, which look like the backs of turtles' shells. These rocks are popular snorkel and dive sites and they experience pretty heavy boat traffic. The reef starts in about 12' of water and runs north to south. Damselfish, angelfish and file fish can be found making their home here but, on more than one occasion spotted eagle rays have been seen cruising through, so keep your eyes open for them.

Date: _____   *Dive #:* _____

Max Depth: _____   *Dive Outfitters:*

Camera: _____

Skill Level: *Lionfish speared:* _____

Notes: _____

_____

_____

_____

_____

_____

_____

_____

Signature: _____

Buddy Signature: _____

Boat Stamp

10) *Big Greenie (Middle Turtle)*

Max Depth: 35 feet

Location: The 2nd or Middle 3rd of Turtle Rocks

Synopsis: Big Greenie is low-profile scattered coral. It gets its name from a massive green brain coral on the site. Schooling grunts and angelfish should keep you company during this dive.

Date: _____   *Dive #:* _____

Max Depth: _____   *Dive Outfitters:* 🤿 ⛵

Camera: _____

Skill Level: ☸   *Lionfish speared:* _____

Notes: _____

_____

_____

_____

_____

_____

_____

_____

_____

Signature: _____

Buddy Signature: _____

Boat Stamp

11) South Turtle Rocks

Max Depth: 35 feet

Location: The Southern 3rd of Turtle Rocks

Synopsis: Near the mooring line is a small boat wreck. The boat was salvaged from the rocks by a couple of Boy Scouts, but their journey was short-lived. The reef starts in about 12' of water and runs north to south. Parrotfish, angelfish and Trumpet fish make their homes here, as well as the occasional spotted eagle ray.

Date: _____   *Dive #:* _____

Max Depth: _____   *Dive Outfitters:* 🛢️ ⛵

Camera: _____

Skill Level: ☸   *Lionfish speared:* _____

Notes: _____

_____

_____

_____

_____

_____

_____

_____

_____

Signature: _____

Buddy Signature: _____

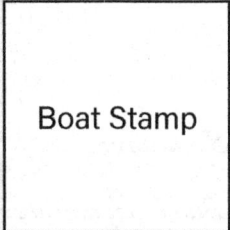

Boat Stamp

12) The Sapona

Max Depth: 20 feet

Location: 4 miles southwest of South Bimini

Synopsis: The Sapona was built by the Liberty Ship Company during WWI as part of a fleet of concrete-hulled ships (because steel was in short supply). The Sapona was completed after the war ended and was sold to Miami developer Carl Fisher, who used the boat as a casino before selling it to rum runner Bruce Bethel in the same year.

During WWII the Sapona's hulking wreck was used as target practice by the U.S. Air Force and Navy. The infamous flight 19 Avenger squadron was returning from a bombing run on the Sapona when they vanished. Then the search and rescue plane sent to find them also disappeared, further perpetuating the myth of the Bermuda Triangle.

Nowadays the Sapona is one of the best dive sites in Bimini. You can spot her haunting skeletal frame sticking out of the water as you pass through Turtle Rocks or Gun Cut. She is deteriorating due to weather and target practice. The ambient light creeping through her offers a great background for photographs, with schools of fish swirling in every direction. On your dive you may find .50 caliber rounds or practice bombs from the Sapona's days as a military target. (Don't worry; the practice bombs are safe!) Schools of grunts, rays, and puffer fish will keep you and your camera busy on this dive for sure.

Date: _____   Dive #: _____

Max Depth: _____   Dive Outfitters: 🛢 ⛵

Camera: _____

Skill Level: ☸   Lionfish speared: _____

Notes: _____

_____

Signature: _____

Buddy Signature: _____

Boat Stamp

13) *Piquet Rocks*

Max Depth: 35 feet

Location: 2 miles south of Turtle Rocks

Synopsis: Low-profile reef with lots of ledges. This area seems prone to visits from sharks so be careful spearfishing here. The reef starts in about 18 feet of water with the deepest part to the west at about 35 feet. Numerous tropical fish species congregate here, including jawfish, angelfish, and parrotfish.

Date: _____   *Dive #:* _____

Max Depth: _____   *Dive Outfitters:*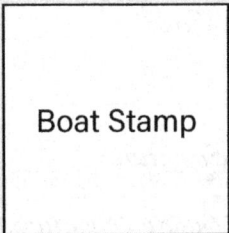

Camera: _____

Skill Level: 🚢   *Lionfish speared:* _____

Notes: _____

_____

_____

_____

_____

_____

_____

_____

_____

_____

Signature: _____

Buddy Signature: _____

Boat Stamp

SOUTH CAT CAY TO RIDING ROCKS

Most of the diving in this area is doable by day boat, but once you start past Ocean Cay toward the Rocks it is probably going to push their travel limit. The area has some amazing sites that are rated year after year among the top ten dives to do in the Bahamas. The sites range from spectacular walls, drifts, and wrecks. This area certainly will not disappoint.

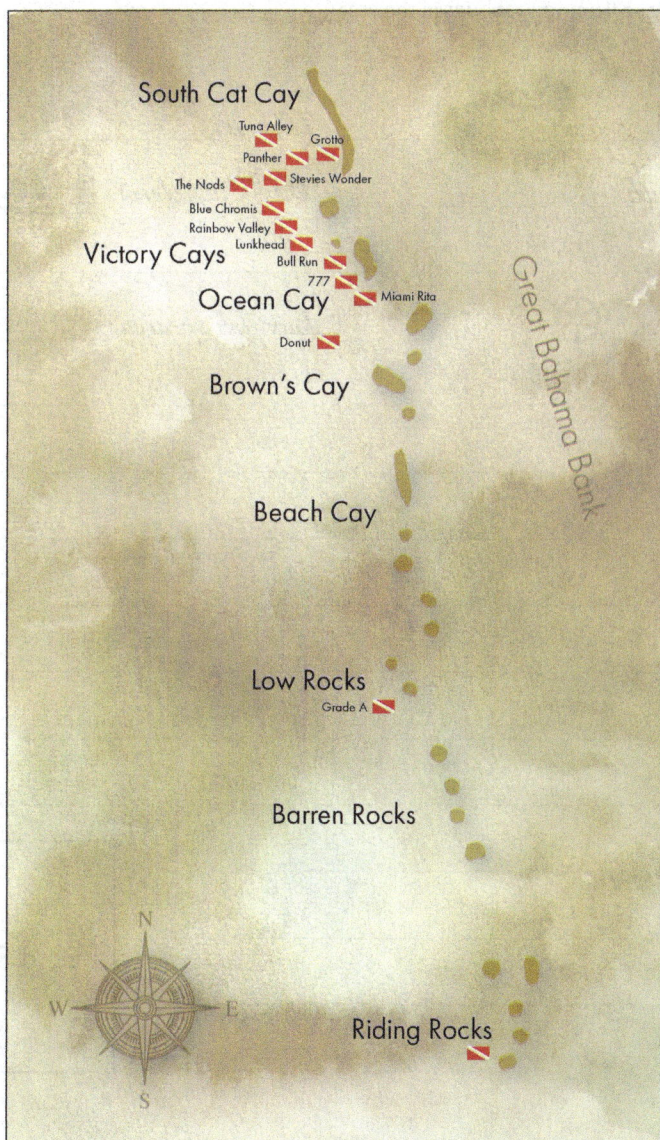

14) *Moxin Rocks (Crotch Rocks)*

Max Depth: 20 feet

Location: 1 mile west, off the southernmost point of Cat Cay

Synopsis: This is a great dive for both beginners and advanced divers. It isn't a large site by any means, but that just means you can focus on the little things. This is one of the few places you'll see flamingo tongues in the area.

Date: _____   *Dive #:* _____

Max Depth: _____   *Dive Outfitters:* 🛢️ ⛵

Camera: _____

Skill Level: ☸   *Lionfish speared:* _____

Notes: _____

_____

_____

_____

_____

_____

_____

_____

_____

_____

Signature: _____

Buddy Signature: _____

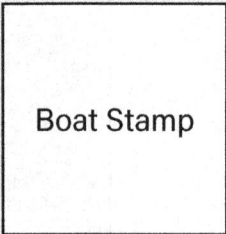

Boat Stamp

15) Tuna Alley
(Aka: Sponge Garden)

Max Depth: 110 feet

Location: 3 miles west of the southern tip of North Cat Cay

Synopsis: The northern portion of the Victory Reef system, which is rated in *Skin Diver* magazine as one of the top ten places to dive in the Bahamas. The reef is named Tuna Alley because, back in the Hemingway era, this is where he supposedly caught those epic 500-pound tuna that decorated the walls at the Compleat Angler. Tuna Alley reef is a high-profile reef with lots of swim-throughs. The reef starts in about 45 feet of water, and slopes off to about 120 feet to the west. It is prone to current and divers have drifted this dive more often than not. The reef is super healthy because the strong current washes away waste products and brings in nutrients. The current is typically northbound. It's not uncommon on a drift to cover over half a mile or more! In the winter months, as you're drifting or diving, keep a lookout into the blue for hammerheads.

Date: _____   Dive #: _____

Max Depth: _____   Dive Outfitters:

Camera: _____

Skill Level: ⚓ ⚓ ⚓   Lionfish speared: _____

Notes: _____

_____

_____

_____

_____

Signature: _____

Buddy Signature: _____

Boat Stamp

16) Stevie's Wonder

Max Depth: 45 feet

Location: 4 miles southwest of the southern tip of South Cat Cay

Synopsis: A reef so beautiful even a blind man could see it! Dive live aboard folklore is that this reef is named after legendary live-aboard dive boat Captain Ray Temeyer's (Lost Island Voyages) son Steve. It is scattered medium-profile coral heads starting in about 20 feet of water. If you drop to the sand you'll find yourself in about 35 feet. Schools of Creole wrasse will part like curtains as you weave through the maze of coral heads. If you make your way to the south you'll probably come across a project by another live-aboard captain, Jim Bob Childs, called Redneck Reef. Not much is left there, but a concrete pig is still getting moved around by the power of the ocean. His name is 'Lil Stubby and is a popular photo op for divers.

Date: _____   Dive #: _____

Max Depth: _____   Dive Outfitters: 🛢️ ⛵

Camera: _____

Skill Level: ☸ ☸   Lionfish speared: _____

Notes: _____

_____

_____

_____

_____

_____

_____

_____

Signature: _____

Buddy Signature: _____

Boat Stamp

17) *The Panther*

Max Depth: 45 feet

Location: 4 miles southwest of the southern tip of South Cat Cay

Synopsis: This is a 45-foot Tug on its side in 40 feet of water. The wreck is not penetrable and has a little growth on it. The coral heads surrounding it offer a chance to see a few fish-cleaning stations. Arrow crabs, goatfish and ocean triggerfish will host your dive. A great dive for novice divers. There are massive amounts of tunicates growing on the wreck.

Date: _____   *Dive #:* _____

Max Depth: _____   *Dive Outfitters:* 🛢️ ⛵

Camera: _____

Skill Level: ☸ ☸   *Lionfish speared:* _____

Notes: _____

_____

_____

_____

_____

_____

_____

_____

_____

_____   Boat Stamp

Signature: _____

Buddy Signature: _____

18) *The Grotto*

Max Depth: 25 feet

Location: 2 miles southwest of the southern tip of South Cat Cay

Synopsis: The rocks are visible from the water and the dive is pretty much up against the rocks. There is a wreck in between the two rocks. It's broken up pretty badly, but there are pieces of metal scattered on the bottom offering great hiding spots for lobsters. Christmas tree worms decorate the rocks. This is a spectacular snorkel or a check dive, and easy to navigate, but watch for surge in rough conditions.

Date: _____   *Dive #:* _____

Max Depth: _____   *Dive Outfitters:*

Camera: _____

Skill Level: 🛞   *Lionfish speared:* _____

Notes: _____

_____

_____

_____

_____

_____

_____

_____

_____

Signature: _____

Buddy Signature: _____

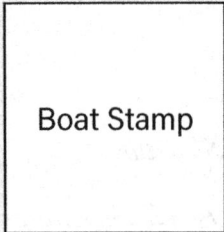

Boat Stamp

19) The Nods

Max Depth: Over the wall

Location: 4 miles southwest of the southern tip of South Cat Cay

Synopsis: One of the premier dives on the Victory Reef system. Starting in about 60 feet of water, the reef runs north to south while sloping off to the deep blue to the west. Because the reef sits on the continental shelf, the Gulf Stream brings in amazing visibility all the while bringing in much-needed nutrients. Again, more often than not this has been a drift dive and considered an advanced dive. Most of the dive is in about 80 feet of water. Schools of pelagics cruise the wall hunting for food. Keep a look out into that blue for hammerheads during the winter months.

Date: _____   *Dive #:* _____

Max Depth: _____   *Dive Outfitters:*

Camera: _____

Skill Level: ⚙ ⚙ ⚙   *Lionfish speared:* _____

Notes: _____

_____

_____

_____

_____

_____

_____

_____

Signature: _____

Buddy Signature: _____

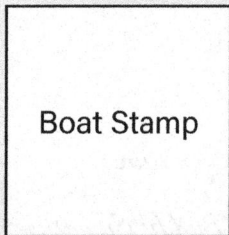

Boat Stamp

20) Blue Chromis

Max Depth: 65 feet

Location: 4 miles southwest of South Cat Cay

Synopsis: This site is prone to current, but because of that it is super healthy. Certainly a great drift with tons of swim-throughs. You will be amazed as you drift over soft corals while huge schools of Blue Chromis part for you. Keep your eyes out for turtles and nurse sharks.

Date: _____   Dive #: _____

Max Depth: _____   Dive Outfitters:

Camera: _____

Skill Level: ⛵ ⛵ ⛵   Lionfish speared: _____

Notes: _____

_____

_____

_____

_____

_____

_____

_____

_____

Signature: _____

Buddy Signature: _____

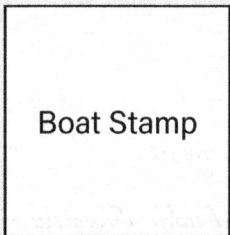

Boat Stamp

21) Rainbow Valley

Max Depth: 50 feet

Location: 4 miles southwest of the southern tip of South Cat Cay

Synopsis: People ask what is my favorite dive near Bimini is, and I think Rainbow Valley is the best dive near Cat Cay! Typically a drift, but if you ever get a chance to do a static dive here, DO IT! There are so many swim-throughs and on good visibility days, you'll get reds well down to 25 feet. Families of scrawl file fish, a resident turtle, and heaps and heaps of Creole wrasse and Chromis make this their home.

Date: _____   Dive #: _____

Max Depth: _____   Dive Outfitters:

Camera: _____

Skill Level: ⚙ ⚙ ⚙   Lionfish speared: _____

Notes: _____

_____

_____

_____

_____

_____

_____

_____

_____

Signature: _____

Buddy Signature: _____

Boat Stamp

22) Lunkhead

Max Depth: 50 feet

Location: 4 miles southwest of the southern tip of South Cat Cay

Synopsis: A huge high-profile coral head coming some 20 feet off the sandy bottom, and surrounded by smaller coral heads. There are tons of brittle stars here making it a spectacular night dive. A huge loggerhead turtle is usually spotted either as you pull up to the site or on the dive. Captain Liza Hash of the Juliet can usually find a pair of octopuses on night dives here. Some of the fish you'll encounter are remoras, Townsend angelfish and parrotfish.

Date: _____   Dive #: _____

Max Depth: _____   Dive Outfitters: 🛢️ ⛵

Camera: _____

Skill Level: ☸️ ☸️   Lionfish speared: _____

Notes: _____

_____

_____

_____

_____

_____

_____

_____   ┌─────────────┐
                                                                    │   │
Signature: _____   │ Boat Stamp │
                                                                    │   │
Buddy Signature: _____   └─────────────┘

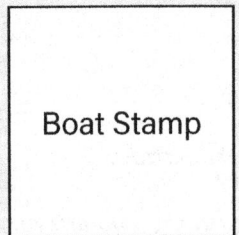

23) *Bull Run*

Max Depth: 60 feet

Location: 4 miles southwest of the southern tip of South Cat Cay

Synopsis: The legendary shark feed site for many live-aboards for many years, though not many dive boats make it down here these days. A few sharks are still hanging around keeping watch. One large one, named Frances by the locals, has a stainless fishing leader hanging from her mouth. The large high-profile coral heads come up about 30 feet from the bottom with many swim-throughs. On the south side in the sand you can spot a rock with a mooring pin sticking out of it. This is where the dive master would send up the float for the chum-sicle for the feed. Garden eels are scattered throughout the sand like sentinels, peeking out occasionally to watch the shark show. Tunicates, spotted filefish, rays, and SHARKS will guide your dive.

Date: _____   *Dive #:* _____

Max Depth: _____   *Dive Outfitters:*

Camera: _____

Skill Level: ✹ ✹ ✹   *Lionfish speared:* _____

Notes: _____

_____

_____

_____

_____

_____

_____

Signature: _____	Boat Stamp
Buddy Signature: _____	

24) 777 (Triple Sevens)

Max Depth: 60 feet

Location: 4 miles southwest of the southern tip of South Cat Cay

Synopsis: A similar profile to Bull Run and just a mere 500 feet from it, so you may still see sharks here. If you are spearfishing be cautious, because the sharks in this area are conditioned to being fed. Scattered high-profile coral heads stick up 30 feet from the sand, which is at about 55-60 feet. Triple Sevens is scattered with swim-throughs, and schools of fish will part as you weave your way through the maze of coral heads here. Garden eels and stingrays decorate the sand outside the coral heads.

Date: _____   Dive #: _____

Max Depth: _____   Dive Outfitters: 🍶 ⛵

Camera: _____

Skill Level: ☸ ☸ ☸   Lionfish speared: _____

Notes: _____

_____

_____

_____

_____

_____

Signature: _____

Buddy Signature: _____

Boat Stamp

25) *Miami-Rita*

Max Depth: 45 feet

Location: 500 feet north of the second green marker going into Ocean Cay

Synopsis: The Miami and the Rita are two tug and a barge that actually collided during a storm. Since they were a hazard to vessels transiting the channel at Ocean Cay, the wrecks were detonated. It is a scattered wreck with nothing to penetrate. It has made an awesome artificial reef and home to rays in the surrounding sand, and lobsters make their home underneath the ledges of steel. One time on this dive, a pod of dolphins actually swam through with the divers. It's an easy site to navigate, but can be prone to current and poor visibility at times.

Date: _____   *Dive #:* _____

Max Depth: _____   *Dive Outfitters:* ⛵

Camera: _____

Skill Level: ☸ ☸   *Lionfish speared:* _____

Notes: _____

_____

_____

_____

_____

_____

_____

_____

Signature: _____

Buddy Signature: _____

Boat Stamp

26) Donut

Max Depth: 45 feet

Location: 4 miles South of Ocean Cay

Synopsis: The surface signature of this reef looks like a Donut, hence the name. The main part of the reef comes up to about 25 feet and drops off to 45' or 50' to the sand. This site is great for lionfish hunting, and scorpion fish can be see here blending in with the reef. There are smaller coral heads to the north of the Donut, about 200' away. This is a great site for novice divers because it's so easy to navigate.

Date: _____   Dive #: _____

Max Depth: _____   Dive Outfitters:

Camera: _____

Skill Level: Lionfish speared: _____

Notes: _____

_____

_____

_____

_____

_____

_____

_____

_____

Signature: _____

Buddy Signature: _____

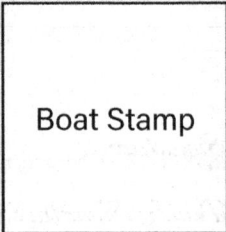

Boat Stamp

27) *Riding Rocks*

Max Depth: 45 feet

Location: 1.5 miles east of Riding Rocks

Synopsis: A sea mound running north and south with smaller coral heads off to each side. There can be a current here from time to time, but it's usually manageable. They say reef sharks don't stop swimming, but two have been spotted laying on the bottom here letting the current wash through their gills. This healthy, beautiful reef is a great spot for lionfish hunting, and is full of small tropicals, angelfish, and lobsters under the ledges.

Date: _____   *Dive #:* _____

Max Depth: _____   *Dive Outfitters:* ⛵

Camera: _____

Skill Level: ☸ ☸   *Lionfish speared:* _____

Notes: _____

_____

_____

_____

_____

_____

_____

_____

_____

Signature: _____

Buddy Signature: _____

Boat Stamp

ORANGE CAY TO THE SANTUREN CHANNEL

There have been many liveaboards that have dived the Orange Cay and Bimini area, but they've either folded or moved to other areas of the Bahamas. Currently there is one liveaboard diving the area consistently, and that is the *Juliet*. She is a three-masted schooner and embodies the true spirit of a live-aboard, diving favorite sites while still daring to explore and check out new ones. Those of you who've dived Orange Cay in previous years will certainly enjoy visiting your old favorites, but if the weather permits, Bimini will open her Santuren Channel secrets to you.

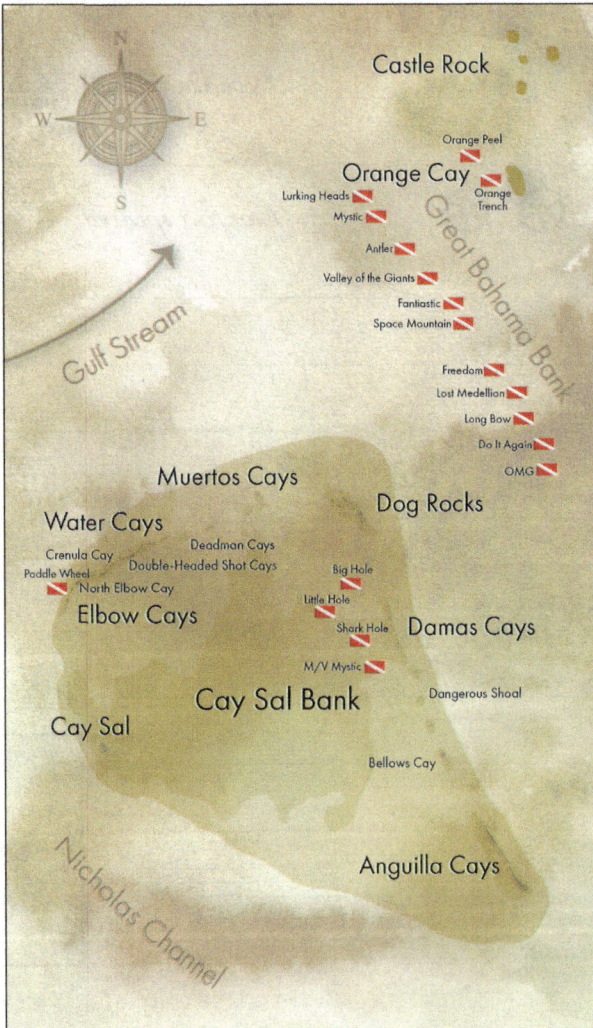

28) Lurking Heads

Max Depth: 60 feet

Location: Orange Cay

Synopsis: Ultra-healthy, scattered, high-profile coral heads starting in about 45 feet of water and dropping to 60 feet at the sand. Schooling jacks, Creole wrasse and the occasional turtle can be found here. You'll definitely want to mind your navigation here; it's easy to move on to the next coral head while drifting in the current. Lobsters will greet you in the openings of ledges. Rays can be found in the sand.

Date: _____   Dive #: _____

Max Depth: _____   Dive Outfitters:

Camera: _____

Skill Level: ⛢ ⛢ ⛢   Lionfish speared: _____

Notes: _____

_____

_____

_____

_____

_____

_____

_____

Signature: _____   Boat Stamp

Buddy Signature: _____

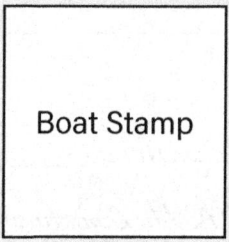

29) *Mystic*

Max Depth: 65 feet

Location: Orange Cay

Synopsis: Less than 1/2 mile away from Lurking Heads, Mystic is a similar dive site offering just as much bountiful beauty. Morays can be found weaving through the holes of the reefs and ledges. The scattered coral heads start at about 35 feet then drop off to 65 feet at the sand. Garden eels and jawfish, along with other small tropicals, will keep you entertained throughout your dive.

Date: _____

Dive #: _____

Max Depth: _____

Dive Outfitters:

Camera: _____

Skill Level: ☸ ☸ ☸

Lionfish speared: _____

Notes: _____

_____

_____

_____

_____

_____

_____

_____

_____

Signature: _____

Buddy Signature: _____

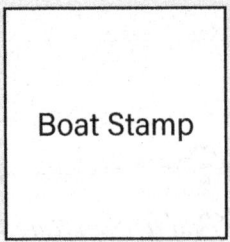

Boat Stamp

30) *Orange Peel*

Max Depth: 30 feet

Location: Orange Cay

Synopsis: A small, low-profile sea mound just a quarter mile off Orange Cay. A super-easy site to navigate and free dive for lobster. Yellow stingrays and larger southern sting rays can be found in the sand. Turtles have been seen on night dives here. Keep your eye out for large French angelfish as well.

Date: _____ *Dive #:* _____

Max Depth: _____ *Dive Outfitters:*

Camera: _____

Skill Level: ✇ ✇ ✇ *Lionfish speared:* _____

Notes: _____

_____

_____

_____

_____

_____

_____

_____

_____

Signature: _____

Buddy Signature: _____

Boat Stamp

31) The Trench

Max Depth: 25 feet

Location: Orange Cay

Synopsis: This is one of those dive sites where people say, "Oh wow, 20 feet," while rolling their eyes, but, there is always a party at the trench, especially for night dives. It's an easy site to navigate. The focal point of the dive is the ledges. They run parallel along Orange Cay and on night dives squid have been spotted here, along with loggerhead turtles and octopi. Definitely want to have your cameras charged for the night dive.

Date: _____ *Dive #:* _____

Max Depth: _____ *Dive Outfitters:* ⛵

Camera: _____

Skill Level: ☸   *Lionfish speared:* _____

Notes: _____

_____

_____

_____

_____

_____

_____

_____

_____

Signature: _____

Buddy Signature: _____

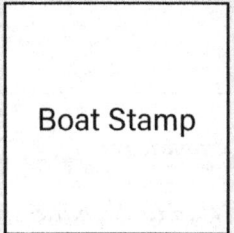

Boat Stamp

32) Antler

Max Depth: 80 feet

Location: Orange Cay

Synopsis: It was once a huge field of stag-horn coral running just under 2 miles, north to south. The coral did suffer some damage from Hurricane Wilma of 2005, but the reef is on the rebound. Large, healthy, high-profile coral heads reach up out of the sand to about 45 feet. Everything can be seen here -- from sharks, to large barrel sponges and queen triggers. There can be current here, but it can also be drifted.

Date: _____   *Dive #:* _____

Max Depth: _____   *Dive Outfitters:* ⛵

Camera: _____

Skill Level: ☸ ☸ ☸   *Lionfish speared:* _____

Notes: _____

_____

_____

_____

_____

_____

_____

_____

_____

Signature: _____

Buddy Signature: _____

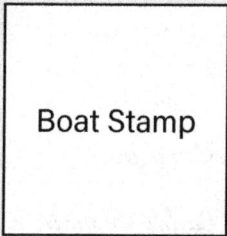

Boat Stamp

33) Valley of the Giants

Max Depth: 80 feet

Location: Orange Cay

Synopsis: Giant high profile coral heads jump up out from the sand. Massive Schools of yellow tail snapper can be found here along with southern and yellow stingrays. This is a great dive for a camera.

Date: _____   Dive #: _____

Max Depth: _____   Dive Outfitters: ⛵

Camera: _____

Skill Level: ☸ ☸ ☸   Lionfish speared: _____

Notes: _____

_____

_____

_____

_____

_____

_____

_____

_____

Signature: _____

Buddy Signature: _____

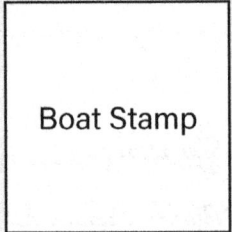

Boat Stamp

34) *Fantastic*

Max Depth: 90 feet

Location: Orange Cay

Synopsis: "Fantastic" definitely lives up to its name. A sea mound peaks at around 40 feet and drops off to about 90 feet at the sandy ocean floor. You'll be greeted by Blue Chromis and an assortment of Wrasses when you enter. Spotted morays and Basslets will keep you entertained as you navigate your way around the site. It's super easy to navigate, since it's one huge coral mound surrounded by sand.

Date: _____   *Dive #:* _____

Max Depth: _____   *Dive Outfitters:*

Camera: _____

Skill Level: ⚙ ⚙ ⚙   *Lionfish speared:* _____

Notes: _____

_____

_____

_____

_____

_____

_____

_____

_____

Signature: _____

Buddy Signature: _____

Boat Stamp

35) *Space Mountain*

Max Depth: 105 feet

Location: Orange Cay

Synopsis: The Disney of dive sites is a large sea mound that starts in about 40 feet then slopes off to about 105 feet to the sand. You can spear lionfish here, but you may also be followed by sharks when doing so. This is one majestic mound that is very healthy. Atlantic Spadefish can be seen circling as you enter the water. You may feel overwhelmed at where to go first and what to follow, but just take your time. Unlike Disney, there are no lines down here! Space Mountain is an easy site to navigate with tons of juvenile and tropical fish to dazzle you during your dive!

Date: _____   *Dive #:* _____

Max Depth: _____   *Dive Outfitters:* ⛵

Camera: _____

Skill Level: ☸ ☸ ☸   *Lionfish speared:* _____

Notes: _____

_____

_____

_____

_____

_____

_____

_____

Signature: _____

Buddy Signature: _____

Boat Stamp

36) *Lost Medallion*

Max Depth: 110 feet

Location: Santuren Channel

Synopsis: Named because a guest jumped in wearing a medallion necklace and lost it during the dive. There have been many searches to find this, but no luck so far. You could be that lucky diver! The reef runs north to south with a maximum depth of 110 feet on the west side and a mountainous profile stretching up to the surface at around 50 feet. There are so many fish here to amaze you, from nurse sharks to blennies.

Date: _____ *Dive #:* _____

Max Depth: _____ *Dive Outfitters:* ⛵

Camera: _____

Skill Level: ☸ ☸ ☸ *Lionfish speared:* _____

Notes: _____

_____

_____

_____

_____

_____

_____

_____

Signature: _____

Buddy Signature: _____

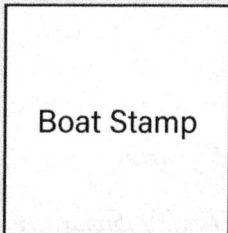

Boat Stamp

37) *Do It Again*

Max Depth: 90 feet

Location: Santuren Channel

Synopsis: Why is it named Do It Again, you ask? Because once you dive this site you're going to want to! It's a football-shaped coral mound that shoots up to around 50 feet. Hundreds of jacks and a few turtles seem to bomb divers from every angle. Bring your camera!

Date: _____   *Dive #:* _____

Max Depth: _____   *Dive Outfitters:* ⛵

Camera: _____

Skill Level: ☸ ☸ ☸   *Lionfish speared:* _____

Notes: _____

_____

_____

_____

_____

_____

_____

_____

_____

Signature: _____

Buddy Signature: _____

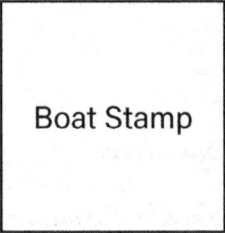

Boat Stamp

38) Freedom Reef

Max Depth: 90 feet

Location: Santuren Channel

Synopsis: Named Freedom Reef because, when it was first discovered, there were abandoned fish traps on the site with live fish in them, which the discovering crew and guests set free. It is a beautiful reef with a dramatic drop-off on the northeast side. Schools of jacks and Atlantic spade fish should keep you entertained while you explore this site.

Date: _____   *Dive #:* _____

Max Depth: _____   *Dive Outfitters:*

Camera: _____

Skill Level: _____   *Lionfish speared:* _____

Notes: _____

_____

_____

_____

_____

_____

_____

_____

_____

Signature: _____

Buddy Signature: _____

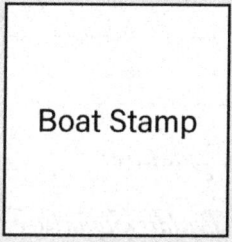

Boat Stamp

39) *Long Bow Reef*

Max Depth: 90 feet

Location: Santuren Channel

Synopsis: Long Bow has it all: healthy coral and heaps of fish in an area that almost looks as if it were a staged aquarium. The reef runs north to south, and is shallow to the eastern side with a dramatic drop-off to the west. Huge schools of jacks, turtles and reef sharks can be seen here. It's also a great lionfish hunting spot.

Date: _____   *Dive #:* _____

Max Depth: _____   *Dive Outfitters:* ⛵

Camera: _____

Skill Level: ☸ ☸ ☸   *Lionfish speared:* _____

Notes: _____

_____

_____

_____

_____

_____

_____

_____

_____

Signature: _____

Buddy Signature: _____

Boat Stamp

40) *O. M. G.*

Max Depth: 80 feet

Location: Santuren Channel

Synopsis: When Divemaster/MarineBio/Captain/All-around great girl Kat Destefano of the *Juliet* jumped in to investigate this site for the first time, she surfaced, spit her regulator out, and shouted, "OMG!" It is a huge high-profile reef system running north to south. You can reach depths around 80 feet to the west and 60 feet or so on the shallow eastern side, with a reef profile topping out around 50 feet. There are lots of Nassau grouper and huge schools of jacks here.

Date: _____ Dive #: _____

Max Depth: _____ Dive Outfitters: ⛵

Camera: _____

Skill Level: ☸ ☸ ☸ Lionfish speared: _____

Notes: _____

_____

_____

_____

_____

_____

_____

Signature: _____

Buddy Signature: _____

Boat Stamp

THE CAY SAL BANK

You want to talk about the stuff legends are made of? Well, look no further than Cay Sal! You have to have a perfect weather window to enjoy the diving in this area. It's 120 nautical miles south of Bimini and only 30 miles from Cuba. It stood in the path of history many times. A CIA-cover oil rig was placed in the center of the bank and was used as a staging ground for the infamous Bay of Pigs invasion. Not long after was the Cuban Missile Crisis. These days it is regularly patrolled by the U.S. Coast Guard for Cuban refugees. The diving has everything from Civil War steamboats, blue holes and even a 200-footfreighter that sank bound for Haiti with medical relief supplies. It is an amazing area to dive!

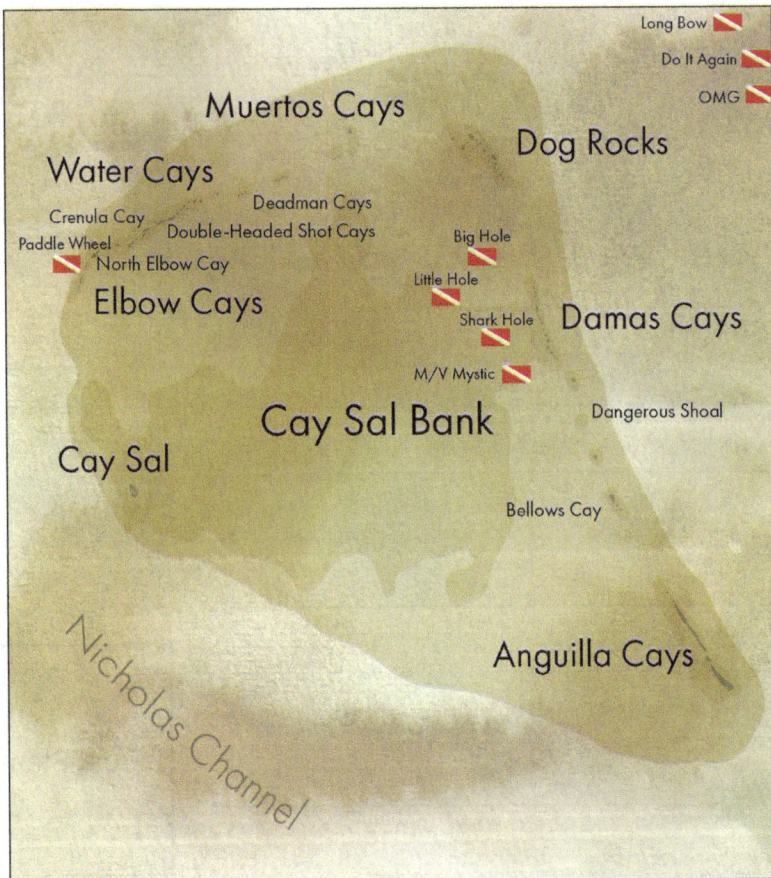

41) *Big Hole*

Max Depth: 130 feet

Location: 1 mile west side of Damas Rocks off the Cay Sal Bank

Synopsis: A beautiful blue hole sitting in about 35 feet of water with a drop-off to God-knows-where inside. The hole is known for sharks and silversides, so take your camera!

Date: _____ *Dive #:* _____

Max Depth: _____ *Dive Outfitters:* ⛵

Camera: _____

Skill Level: ☸ ☸ *Lionfish speared:* _____

Notes: _____

_____

_____

_____

_____

_____

_____

_____

_____

_____

_____

Signature: _____

Buddy Signature: _____

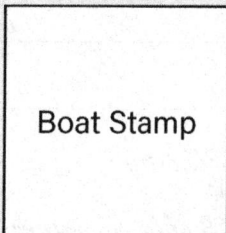

Boat Stamp

42) *Black Hole*

Max Depth: 130 feet

Location: West Side Damas Rocks, Cay Sal Bank

Synopsis: A smaller hole just southeast of Damas Rocks. Recently, there was a lot of debris from a wreck scattered around the outskirts of the hole. It's still a great dive to check out, with tons of silversides to keep you busy.

Date: _____   *Dive #:* _____

Max Depth: _____   *Dive Outfitters:*

Camera: _____

Skill Level: ⚓ ⚓   *Lionfish speared:* _____

Notes: _____

_____

_____

_____

_____

_____

_____

_____

_____ | Boat Stamp |

Signature: _____

Buddy Signature: _____

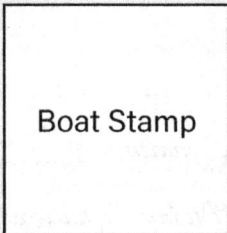

43) The M/V Mystic

Max Depth: 35 feet

Location: West Side Damas Rocks, Cay Sal Bank

Synopsis: If you get to the western edge of Cay Sal you have to check out the Mystic Wreck. It is a 206-foot freighter that struck a submerged rock in heavy weather en route to Haiti with earthquake relief supplies. They sent out a mayday and the USCG came and rescued all 10 people (and the dog) on board. The boat is broken in two pieces and the super-structure was peeking out of the water. On afternoon and night dives, turtles come in to say hello.

Date: _____ *Dive #:* _____

Max Depth: _____ *Dive Outfitters:* ⛵

Camera: _____

Skill Level: ☸ ☸ ☸   *Lionfish speared:* _____

Notes: _____

_____

_____

_____

_____

_____

_____

_____

_____

Boat Stamp

Signature: _____

Buddy Signature: _____

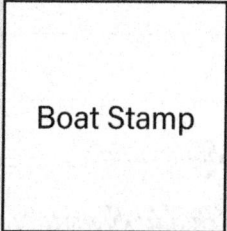

44) The Paddle Wheel Steamer

Max Depth: 35 feet

Location: West side of Elbow Cay, north of the lighthouse

Synopsis: Sitting in 35 feet of water is a paddle wheel steamer just off to the north of the lighthouse. The area is picturesque and the wreck is covered in fairy basslets and blue chromis. Some say the wreck is an old blockade runner and others say it was a mail boat en route from Nassau to Wilmington, NC, a popular trade route. For now it's just another mystery for us to speculate on.

Date: _____ Dive #: _____

Max Depth: _____ Dive Outfitters:

Camera: _____

Skill Level: ⚙ ⚙   Lionfish speared: _____

Notes: _____

_____

_____

_____

_____

_____

_____

_____

_____

Signature: _____

Buddy Signature: _____

Boat Stamp

UNDERWATER PHOTOGRAPHY AND VIDEO

*I*f you are looking for a way to document your dives and share your experiences with your friends on social media then underwater photography is what you are looking for -- especially for those who make a hobby trying to identify different species of fish. A digital photograph will certainly help you since so many fish closely resemble each other. It is not hard to spend a king's ransom on underwater photography equipment but there are a lot of affordable options out there that take amazing pictures.

When choosing an underwater camera and housing, two things to consider are size and weight. If you are a beginner I recommend going with a compact camera such as a GoPro, Olympus Tough or a Sealife. IPhones now have an underwater housing rated for 130 feet and take amazing pictures. I use these models for a lot of reasons, the main reason being size. The weight restrictions put on bags by airlines are a struggle for divers and these cameras are small, lightweight and can certainly get the job done. Remember bigger isn't always better. Aside from the weight issue, remember sometimes we have to climb out of the water back onto a boat in rough seas with it and a small camera is easier to handle.

A lot of compact cameras are self-contained these days, even Go Pros, meaning that the camera requires no external housing. If your camera is an older model GoPro, it does require some maintenance and care,but it is pretty straightforward. You just have to remember to make sure that before you close that housing the o-rings are clear and not pinched, and are covered in a light silicone grease. A good way to check your housing is to just take it on a dive without the camera inside to depth. When you are back on the surface from your dive, open your housing and it should be dry. I especially recommend this if you are using the iPhone housing, not because they are prone to leaking, but because so much of our lives are on our phones these days.

One of the most frustrating obstacles for new underwater photographers is how quickly water absorbs light. Water is much more dense than air and absorbs light quickly. This results in dull images with a blue/grey hue to them. There are a couple approaches to compensating for this problem and reintroducing light and colors back into your photos.

Certain colors get absorbed at certain depths. Starting from the longest to the shortest wavelength: red is the first to go at around 15 feet, then orange at 30 feet, yellow at 60 feet, green at 90 feet and finally blue at 120 feet. Due to the loss of these colors at depth we must compensate and one of the easiest ways to do this is by adding artificial light or a camera flash.

External lights and flashes can be purchased for most compact cameras and will artificially reintroduce colors and sharpness back into your photos, showing all the vibrant colors of the reef and its creatures. If your camera already has a flash or you are using an external flash you will want to get a diffuser to soften the light. Make sure you use a diffuser if possible because without one photos tend to look washed out.

During day dives, a red filter is an inexpensive way to help get colors back into your photos. They are specifically designed for different depths to compensate for all colors lost by water density. You will want to check to make sure your camera or housing is compatible for one. For GoPros they can usually be purchased for around $15. I usually attach my filter to the camera or housing after I am under water to prevent air bubbles from popping up between the lens and filter.

Once you have your equipment sorted out, let's talk about underwater photo etiquette. If you are just starting out as a diver I cannot stress this enough, but you should have your buoyancy under control. It should be as natural as breathing. Taking pictures has us hyper-focused on our subjects and divers who have a problem with buoyancy often end up clanging into the reefs and or other divers. You do not want to be that person on a dive boat! So PLEASE make sure you are comfortable with your buoyancy. Also, if you are using a light or strobe avoid shining it in other divers' eyes, especially on night dives!

GUIDELINES FOR GREAT PHOTOS

1) Know how to dive and know how to dive well. Having control of your buoyancy should be second nature when it comes to taking underwater photos or videos. If you do not have this skill mastered, you pose a threat to yourself and the reef around you, and you risk ruining other people's dives. Also, it's easy to lose track of time and air consumption while looking for that perfect photo. So remember the basic diving fundamentals like your depth, dive time and air consumptions. No photo is worth getting decompression sickness over.

2) Get close to your subject carefully, and when you think you are close enough get closer. This is a very difficult task, but you will find as you become a better diver you will be able to get closer to your subject without spooking it. This will be accomplished by being a relaxed diver and letting the marine life get used to you. Some of the best underwater photographers I have seen actually wait for the marine life to approach them.

3) Patience is key and prepare to take a lot of photos. Remember it does not cost money to push the capture button on your camera. Experiment with different lights and camera settings and review each one -- it will speed up your learning curve for taking pictures.

4) Try not to ever shoot downwards so your perspective is a little more than just the sea bottom. Most photos taken from above the subject end up blending into to the reef and it is difficult to determine what the photo is actually supposed to be. Separation is the name of the game. Some exceptions to this would be sharks or turtles with contrasting sandy bottoms.

5) Have spares of both chargers and batteries and be sure batteries are charged before a dive briefing is called.

6) Do not harass marine life! If the subject is clearly bothered by your presence and light especially leave it alone. You would not want

someone barging into your home while you sleep shining a bright light in your eyes.

UNDERWATER VIDEO GUIDELINES

1) The same guidelines that apply for photos also apply underwater videos. People are mesmerized by videos and it is a great way to tell a story of your dive vacation. You can thrill your friends with a video of a shark feed and the wonderful underwater world. Most compact cameras have a video setting that can shoot high definition video. When shooting video, I usually use a filter instead of an external light on day dives because most of your shots are wide angle and it is hard to find an external light powerful enough to light up a large area.

2) Shoot in sequences if you are going to upload a video for social media -- you will want to keep your video less than two minutes. Think of your video as a highlight reel and try to plan these sequences before your dive. You can ask your buddy to model or star in your video.

3) Keep the movement of the video constant and steady. Position yourself on one side of the reef or wreck and have your buddy swim towards you while you stay still taking video. This usually pushes marine life towards you, making a great shot.

4) Try looking over at the top of your camera at your subject. Most viewing windows on cameras are really small and difficult to look through while taking videos underwater and often end up looking shaky.

EDITING YOUR VIDEOS

Video editing is a very tedious but fun and rewarding process. The idea of shooting in sequences is to make the editing process easier. Most camera and computers today have their own editing software making it easy for you to edit your video. The software gives you the ability to add titles, transitions and even add a music track, giving your dive video a professional and polished look. Take a look of some of your favorite underwater videos on YouTube and try to mimic their techniques. Eventually you'll develop your own style and wow your friends with great dive videos.

WIDE ANGLE OR MACRO?

Wide angle photos are probably the most common photos taken under water. The wide angle setting or lens will give you perspective shots of swim-throughs, action shots of divers, shark feeds, shipwrecks and diver and marine life interaction. Perspective shots taken with wide angle lenses or settings tend to give the person looking at the photo a feel for a scene or setting. An example is this photo of a diver surrounded by high profile coral admiring a turtle with a deep blue backdrop.

Macro lenses or settings are used when you are close to your subject. This is probably one of the easier and more rewarding aspects of under water photography because it opens your eyes up to a whole new world of tiny creatures that inhabit the sea and reefs. Macro settings or lenses magnify your subject many times and you start looking for subjects that are typically not seen during regular dives. You will quickly find that dives you once found boring are now havens for amazing creatures like juvenile fish, Flamingo Tongue or Christmas tree worms.

THINGS YOU CAN DO IF YOUR CAMERA HOUSING FLOODS.

Every underwater photographer's worst nightmare is probably a camera housing flooding. Most scuba divers are in far-reaching, remote places, so the odds of finding a camera repair shop are probably next to none. I am going to warn you, there probably isn't much hope for you in this situation, but you can take some steps that may get you up and running again.

1: If you're using an external housing and you notice it begins to leak while on a dive, try to power the camera off and surface safely.

2: Once on the surface remove your SD card and battery.

3: Dunk the camera quickly in fresh water.

4: If 99% isopropyl rubbing alcohol is available submerge your camera in it quickly.

5: If rice is available, put some in a zipper lock bag large enough to bury the camera. Set it in a warm, sunny place for at least 24 hours. The rice will help absorb what moisture the alcohol did not evaporate.

6: Try powering the camera up with a back up battery or power cord and hopefully you're up and running again.

Again, none of these are guarantees but will help improve your odds of saving your equipment. If you purchased trip insurance, check to see whether these types of losses are covered. Most manufacturer warranties are voided due to water damage but it never hurts to check.

COMPLETE DIVE OPERATIONS DIRECTORY: BAHAMAS

*I*f you are looking to dive other areas of the Bahamas, here is a complete directory of dive operations.

ISLAND: ABACOS

Operator: Brendal's Dive Center & Water Sports International
Email: brendal@brendal.com
Website: www.brendal.com
Reservations: (242) 365-4411

Operator: DIVE ABACO!
Email: dive@diveabaco.com
Website: www.DiveAbaco.com
Reservations: (800)247-5338

Operator: Dive Guana
Email: diveguana@yahoo.com
Website: www.diveguana.com
Reservations: (242) 365-5178

Operator: Dive Time
Email: info@divetimeabaco.com
Website: www.divetimeabaco.com
Reservations: 2423656235

Operator: Froggies Out Island Adventure, Ltd.
Email: dive@froggiesabaco.com
Website: www.froggiesabaco.com
Reservations: (242) 366-0431

Operator: Treasure Cay Resort
Email: skappeler@treasurecay.com
Website: www.treasurecay.com
Reservations: (242) 365-8801

ISLAND: ANDROS ISLAND

Operator: Small Hope Bay Lodge
Email: shbmkt@smallhope.com
Website: www.SmallHope.com
Reservations: (800) 223-6961

Operator: Tiamo Resort
Email: reservations@tiamoresorts.com
Website: www.tiamoresorts.com
Reservations: (242) 369-2330

ISLAND: BIMINI ISLANDS

Operator: Bimini Big Game Club
PADI Dive Center
Email: dive@biggameclubbimini.com
Website: www.biggameclubbimini.com
Reservations: (800) 867-4764

Operator: Neal Watsons Bimini
Scuba Center
Email: dive@biminisands.com
Website: www.biminisands.com
Reservations: (800) 737-1007

Operator: Bimini Undersea
Email: ebriones68@gmail.com
Website: www.biminiundersea.com
Reservations: (786) 462-4641

LIVEABOARD OPERATORS - NASSAU AND EXUMAS

Operator: Aqua Cat Cruises
Email: bda@aquacatcruises.com
Website: www.aquacatcruises.com
Reservations: (888) 327-9600

Operator: Cat Ppalu Cruises
Email: bda@catppalu.com
Website: www.catppalu.com
Reservations: (800) 327-9600

Operator: Blackbeard's Cruises
Email: bda@blackbeard-cruises.com
Website: www.blackbeard-cruises.com
Reservations: (800) 327-9600

Operator: Sea Dragon (Exuma Cays,
Conception Island)
Email: seadragonbahamas@hotmail.com
Website: www.seadragonbahamas.com
Reservations: (954) 522-0161

Operator: Carib Dancer (Part of the
worldwide Dancer Fleet)
Email: carib@dancerfleet.com
Website: www.DancerFleet.com
Reservations: (800) 932-6237

Operator: Lost Island Voyages
Email: Info@lostislandvoyages.com
Website: www.lostislandvoyages.com
Reservations: (305) 756-7762

ISLAND: EXUMA ISLANDS

Operator: Dive Exuma
Email: diveexuma@hotmail.com
Website: www.dive-exuma.com
Reservations: (242) 357-0313

ISLAND: GRAND BAHAMA / FREEPORT

Operator: Deep Water Cay
Email: CPipes@DeepWaterCay.com
Website: www.deepwatercay.com
Reservations: (970) 283-9420

Operator: UNEXSO
Email: info@Unexso.com
Website: www.unexso.com
Reservations: (800) 992-3483

Operator: Sunn Odyssey Divers
Email: karen@sunnodysseydivers.com
Website: www.sunnodysseydivers.com
Reservations: (242) 373-4014

ISLAND: HARBOUR ISLAND, ELEUTHERA

Operator: Valentine's Dive Center
Email: dive@valentinesdive.com
Website: www.valentinesdive.com
Reservations: (242) 333-2080

ISLAND: LONG ISLAND

Operator: Stella Maris Watersports
Email: ian@stellamariswatersports.com
Website: www.stellamariswatersports.com
Reservations: (800) 426-0466

ISLAND: NEW PROVIDENCE / NASSAU

Operator: Bahama Divers
Email: bahpro@hotmail.com
Website: www.bahamadivers.com
Reservations: (866) 662-7728

Operator: Nassau Paradise Island
   Promotion Board
Email: kristin@npipb.com
Website: www.nassauparadiseisland.
   com/what-to-do/watersports
Reservations: (954) 888-5913

Operator: Stuart Cove's Dive
   Bahamas
Email: info@stuartcove.com
Website: www.stuartcove.com
Reservations: (888) 357-4275

ISLAND: SAN SALVADOR

Operator: Riding Rock Resort
Email: info@ridingrock.com
Website: www.ridingrock.com
Reservations: (800) 272-1492

Operator: Seafari Bahamas @ Club Med
Email: Bahamas@seafari-int.com
Website: www.seafari-int.com
   /bahamas_fr.html
Reservations: (242) 331-2000

BIBLIOGRAPHY

Gerace, Donald T., ed. *Columbus and His World*. Proc. of First San Salvador Conference, College Center of the Finger Lakes, Bahamas. N.p.: n.p., n.d. Print.

Higginson, Thomas Wentworth. *Tales of the Enchanted Islands of the Atlantic*. New York: Macmillan, 1899. Print.

Finkelman, Paul. *Encyclopedia of African American History: 1896 to the Present: From the Age of Segregation to the Twenty-first Century*. Oxford: Oxford UP, 2009. Print.

"The Union Blockade of the Southern States." *The Union Blockade of the Southern States - Essential Civil War Curriculum*. N.p., n.d. Web. 21 Apr. 2017.

Coker, John. *Sun, Sea and Lights: The Memoirs of an Inspector of the Imperial Lighthouse Service*. UK: Publisher Not Identified, 2009. Print.

"Martin Luther King, Jr. Pilgrimage." *Martin Luther King, Jr. Pilgrimage - The Bahamas Family of Islands*. Bahamas Ministry of Tourism, n.d. Web. 21 Apr. 2017.

Allen, Kevin. "Bimini Suffered Hangover When Illicit Party Ended." *Tribunedigital-sunsentinel*. Sun Sentinel, 13 Mar. 1988. Web. 26 Apr. 2017.

Cummings, Greg. "Pirate Yarns." *Drug Smugglers Use High-Speed Boats to Run Cocaine, Marijuana Into Florida.* N.p., 01 Jan. 1970. Web. 21 Apr. 2017.

Nordheimer, Jon. "POLICE CORRUPTION PLAGUING FLORIDA." *The New York Times.* The New York Times, 02 Aug. 1986. Web. 26 Apr. 2017.

Meek, Alison. "Murders and Pastels in Miami: The Role of "Miami Vice" in Bringing Back Tourists to Miami." 90.3 (2012): 286-305. Web. 26 Apr. 2017.

Fisheries, NOAA. "Invasive Lionfish Threaten Coral Reefs and Fisheries." *NOAA Fisheries.* N.p., 15 Dec. 2014. Web. 24 Apr. 2017.

Harrell, Scott. "Eating Lionfish - Can You Eat Lionfish & How Do I Cook Lionfish?" *Eating Lionfish.* Lionfish Hunting, 2017. Web. 24 Apr. 2017.

TheScottHarrell. "Lionfish Sting First Aid Treatment | Envenomation Response and Care." *Lionfish Hunting.* N.p., n.d. Web. 26 Apr. 2017.

"Scrawled Filefish." *Answers in Genesis.* N.p., n.d. Web. 24 Apr. 2017.

Castro, Joseph. "Must Sharks Keep Swimming to Stay Alive?" *LiveScience.* Purch, 28 May 2013. Web. 24 Apr. 2017.

"S.S. Sapona." *Power & Motoryacht.* N.p., n.d. Web. 26 Apr. 2017.

ABOUT THE AUTHOR

*C*aptain Nathan (Nate) Riley has been around boats since his early teens when he helped his stepfather prepare for a transatlantic crossing from California to Scotland. He began working on boats professionally in 2001 as a 26-year-old sailboat captain. He crossed the Gulf Stream weekly from Miami, FL to the Bahamas and participated in organized shark feeds. Since then, sailing has taken him all over the world—from Alaska to the Gulf of Mexico to his current stop, the Bahamas and Virgin Islands.

Capt. Nate is an avid scuba diver who loves underwater photography. He spends about nine months out of the year at sea and loves to share his passion for the open water not only with fellow sailors, but also with new and seasoned divers alike. For him, it's about sending his guests back home relaxed and smiling.

When he isn't sailing on the high seas, Capt. Nate resides in Ocala, FL where he can be found running marathons or trail running through the Ocala National Forest. His favorite hobbies—aside from sailing—are writing, making dinner for his family, and babysitting his two grandchildren.

Check out Capt. Nate Riley's photography and adventures on Facebook under "Nate's Captain's Blog."

Made in the USA
Coppell, TX
12 November 2025

63018426R00089